SEVEN

ways to increase your

ANOINTING

GLENN AREKION

DESTINY IMAGE™ EUROPE srl
Via Maiella, 1
66020 San Giovanni Teatino (Ch) - Italy

"Changing the world, one book at a time."

This book and all other Destiny Image™ Europe books are available at Christian bookstores and distributors worldwide.

To order products, or for any other correspondence:

DESTINY IMAGE™ EUROPE srl
Via Acquacorrente, 6
65123 - Pescara - Italy
Tel. +39 085 4716623 - Fax +39 085 9431270
E-mail: info@eurodestinyimage.com

Or reach us on the Internet: www.eurodestinyimage.com

ISBN: 978-88-89127-84-1
For Worldwide Distribution, Printed in the U.S.A.
1 2 3 4 5 6 7 8/13 12 11 10 09

DEDICATION

This book is dedicated to Reverend Lindsey James Mann. I thank you, Sir, for being my principal, pastor, and friend. Thank you for pushing and stretching me. I will always treasure the lessons I learned from you. We no longer live in the same nation, but I always bless the Lord for your input in my life. Your investment in me is far greater than anything money could buy.

TABLE OF CONTENTS

INTRODUCTION

The greatest travesty in the twenty-first century modern church is that we profess Christ but in reality are not acquainted with His power. As you look around today, you will see that iniquity is on the rise. The apostle Paul stated many years ago that where sin abounds grace will abound much more. Grace is the power of God.

It is time for you to rise up. The earnest of creation is waiting for the manifestation of the sons of God. This is your time to be manifested in this world that desperately needs the demonstration of the power of God. This book is written with you, the believer or minister, in mind. It is time for a change in your life. As much as we love great orators, the church and the world need more. The church is ready for some fresh blood that has been touched by God's power. There is, however, a price to pay for God's power. No man can display power from on high without first having paid a price. His power and anointing are available to you.

What you are about to read will revolutionize your life to a higher dimension. In these days of apostasy and deception, the church and the world are ready for genuine power and faith. The apostle Paul was certain that Timothy, his son in the faith, walked in unfeigned faith.

"When I call to remembrance the unfeigned faith that is in thee, which dwelt first in thy grandmother Lois, and thy mother Eunice; and I am persuaded that in thee also" (2 Tim. 1:5).

Unfeigned is also rendered as sincere, true, and genuine. We are ready for a genuine and true move of God. You can be the catalyst for a great revival in your church, community, and country. However there is a price to pay. If you are willing to pay the price then you shall obtain the prize.

What is the price?

We have heard it said over and over again by ministers and well-meaning believers, "Well, brother, there is a price to pay for God's anointing!" Unfortunately, that's all we hear. No one ever tells us specifically what the price is. We cannot appropriate that which we do not know. Only after enquiring and knowing you have sufficient information can you then appropriate the goods.

The Devil's Worst Nightmare

But my horn shalt thou exalt like the horn of an unicorn [wild ox]: *I shall be anointed with fresh oil* (Psalm 92:10).

God brought them out of Egypt; he hath as it were the strength of an unicorn [wild ox]. *Surely there is no enchantment against Jacob, neither is there any divination against Israel: according to this time it shall be said of Jacob and of Israel, What hath God wrought! Behold, the people shall rise up as a great lion, and lift up himself as a young lion: he shall not lie down until he eat of the prey, and drink the blood of the slain* (Numbers 23:22-24).

His glory [Joseph] *is like the firstling of his bullock, and his horns are like the horns of unicorns: with them he shall push the people together to the ends of the earth: and they are the ten thousands of Ephraim, and they are the thousands of Manasseh* (Deuteronomy 33:17).

Say it out loud: "I am anointed with fresh oil and I am a wild ox." I love Darby's rendition of Psalm 92:10, which says, "But my horn

shalt thou exalt like a buffalo's: I shall be anointed with fresh oil."
This is what a fresh anointing will make you into a wild ox or a wild
buffalo. My horn will be exalted! The anointing is a promoter! When
the Bible talks about a horn, it refers to position and strength. In fact,
it refers to supernatural strength that elevates one position. God will
exalt your position like the horn of a unicorn. The literal Hebrew
translation says, "like the horn of a wild ox." The ox typifies strength,
service, and patience.

The problem with the church today is that we have too many
tame, civilized oxen who are plowing the devil's field, of shame and
reproach. Satan has yoked millions of believers with infirmities, and
they just sit there as victims of their circumstances. Many do not even
anticipate a life of victory but only of despair, hoping for the sweet by
and by to get here in a hurry. A man once told me, "Yes, brother
Glenn, we are helpless pilgrims here. This is our life, treading
through the heat and the cold. What can we do about it?"

I will tell you what we can do about it. First, we can stop this unbelief and blasphemy before God. We are not helpless pilgrims; we
are God's children, anointed with fresh oil. We are wild oxen. It is
time that we started acting like wild oxen rather than weak, insipid,
and dejected creatures.

If you are born again, the anointing of God is in you. It is time to
start rebelling against every assignment of the devil. A wild ox en-
joys freedom of movement and rebels against restrictions. If you
put a yoke on a wild ox, he will kick it off and go after you. Look at
what God said to Job: "Will the wild ox be willing to serve you, or
remain beside your manger? Can you bind the wild ox with a har-
ness to the plow in the furrow? Or will he harrow the furrows for
you?" (Job 39:9-10 AMP). The wild ox is not willing to serve, and
neither should you be willing to serve the devil. You cannot bind a
wild ox. Make up your mind from today that the devil will no longer
be able to bind you in unusual circumstances.

As a wild ox, freshly anointed, you are the devil's worst nightmare, just as Jesus was. Our Lord was anointed with the Holy
Ghost and power, and the Bible says He went about doing good and

healing all those who were oppressed of the devil. Jesus' very first words in a sermon were, "The Spirit of the Lord is upon me because *He hath anointed me* to preach the gospel...to heal...to deliver and set at liberty" (Luke 4:18). The very focus of that anointing was beamed against satan's oppression. Jesus became the oppressor of the oppressor! Look at the boldness of Jesus, who said, "The prince of this world cometh, and hath nothing in me" (John 14:30). The Message version of this same scripture says, "The chief of this godless world is about to attack. But don't worry—*he has nothing on me, no claim on me.*"

When you realize you are anointed like a wild ox, you will also declare that satan has nothing on you and no claim on your life. Even if a chief wizard comes against you and casts a spell on you, it will not work. God has already said concerning the wild ox, "Surely there is no enchantment and no divination against Jacob" (Numbers 23:23). The Message version says it this way, "No magic spells can bind Jacob, no incantations can hold back Israel." The Good News Bible makes it even clearer, "There is no magic charm, no witchcraft, that can be used against the nation of Israel." The New Living Translation says, "No curse can touch Jacob; no magic has any power against Israel."

This is shouting ground! No assignment or plan of satan can touch you, for you are a wild ox! A wild ox is not afraid of witches, spells, or incantations. As it was prophesied over Joseph, it is true for you: "His horns will push" (Deut. 33:17). Push your way into victory!

Push all fear out of your life! Push diseases out of your life! Push generational curses out of your life! Kick every assignment off and out of your life! You can do it. Let's get ready to increase in the anointing.

Chapter 1

ONE SATURDAY MORNING
IN LOUISVILLE

Ever since I was born again, Friday night has been "prayer meeting" night. In my early days as a believer in London, the prayer meeting was fondly called "All Night." We would say, "Are you going to All Night tonight?" I was fourteen years old when I attended my first "All Night prayer meeting." At the All Night, we prayed from 11:00 P.M. to 5:00 A.M. Although in the early days I would fall asleep on the floor while we were praying, I can confidently tell you that these prayer meetings changed my young life for the better. Waiting upon the Lord Jesus Christ, praying in tongues for long periods of time, and the strong teaching we received formed and fashioned me for life and ministry.

It was in these prayer meetings that I first knew I would spend a lot of time in Nigeria. God put that desire in my heart. It was also in these prayer meetings that God rekindled my fire and passion for America. That is why my main focus in life is America and Nigeria. These are the two places where I am most effective. We are most effective in the place where God has assigned and commissioned us.

You must understand that you are not to go wherever and whenever you please, even though it may be within your power, but you are to go where God sends you. There is a place for you where you will see the mighty hand of God over your life. This is a very simple principle, but many have not understood it and have made a shipwreck of their lives. The apostle Paul was commissioned to the Gentiles and Peter to the Jewish people.

In his epistle to the Galatians, Paul declared, "But contrariwise, when they saw that the gospel of the uncircumcision was committed unto me, as the gospel of the circumcision was unto Peter; (For he that wrought *effectually* in Peter to the apostleship of the circumcision, the same was *mighty* in me toward the Gentiles)" (Gal. 2:7,8). Pay special attention to the words *effectually* and *mighty*. Both words mean the same thing! It is the Greek word *energeo*, and it means to be operative, to put forth power, or to display power. The anointing is a display or showing of power or God's energy. The power was on display in their respective places and callings.

However, Paul had all kinds of problems every time he stepped outside his calling and anointing. Someone has said, "I can go everywhere because God said to go into all the world to preach the Gospel." That is a true statement but it is to the entire Church or Body of Christ, not just to an individual. As a believer or minister, we have to know where God has sent us so we can be fruitful. "Now when they had gone throughout Phrygia and the region of Galatia, and *were forbidden of the Holy Ghost* to preach the word in Asia. After they were come to Mysia, they assayed to go into Bithynia: but the Spirit suffered them not" (Acts 16:6-7).

The Great Commission applied to Paul too, so why did the Holy Spirit stop him from going to Asia? Paul was to go where the Holy Spirit guided him to go:

> And a vision appeared to Paul in the night; there stood a man of Macedonia, and prayed him, saying, Come over into Macedonia, and help us. And after he had seen the vision, immediately we endeavored to go into Macedonia, assuredly gathering that the Lord had called us for to preach the gospel unto them. Therefore loosing from Troas, we came with a straight course to Samothracia, and the next day to Neapolis (Acts 16:9-11).

You always want to be in the center of God's will so that you can see His mighty power at work in your life. God's power and anointing will be on display and increased in your life when you are in the place where He has appointed you. To know that place of increase, you will definitely have to wait upon Him for instruction and direction.

What you are about to read will revolutionize your life to a higher dimension. As I mentioned earlier, we spent long hours praying in tongues on Friday nights. The contents for this book came to me on a Saturday morning after our Friday prayer meeting in Louisville, Kentucky. I woke up that morning and heard these words ringing loud in my spirit. "Meditation, petition, consecration, association, impartation...will increase the anointing." I quickly jotted them down in my notepad and then went downstairs to my prayer room.

As I thought about those words, I knew there must be more. As I spent some more time praying in tongues, I knew the Holy Spirit wanted to reveal more of the ways to increasing the anointing in my life. (I make no apology for being a tongue-talker. It is the greatest power in the universe. We'll discuss that when we talk about petition.) As I kept praying in tongues, I drew by the Holy Spirit these words from my spirit, "meditation, petition, consecration, association, impartation, adoration, and dedication...will increase the anointing." If you are tired of powerless Christianity and want to see the power of God in your life and the weakness of the devil, fasten your seat belt for the ride of your life. "And Jesus returned in the power of the Spirit into Galilee" (Luke 4:14).

Powerlessness is rampant in the church today. The chief reason for our powerlessness is our refusal to pay the price for God's supernatural power. Now please understand, I am not talking about salvation. Jesus paid the price for that on Calvary's cross, and we are recipients of the paid price. However there is a price to pay for the power of God to flow out of our lives! Whatever price *you* pay will determine what will come into *your* life! The price determines the prize. There is no cheap access to the power of God. It is available to "whosoever," but it will cost you something.

I remember watching a television documentary about India, and the program showed a man who separated himself from his family, lived like a hobo in a cemetery, and ate from the skull of a dead person, all in his quest for spiritual power. No doubt you have heard or read about what witches and warlocks do to gain spiritual and demonic power. Even the wicked know that spiritual power, whether from God or demons, comes at a price.

The apostle Paul was someone who went for the high prize in his calling, as he stated in his letter to the Philippian saints: "And reaching forth unto those things which are before, I press toward the mark for the prize of the high calling of God in Christ Jesus" (Phil. 3:13-14). Many have refused to pay the price of the high calling but instead have turned to psychology and other man-made philosophies to bring deliverance to people. No wonder the church is weak today! New creation realities are substituted for *secular* humanistic psychology that further amplifies the problem. Where are the great miracles, signs, and wonders that Jesus said would follow the believers? "And *these signs* shall follow them that believe; in My name shall they cast out devils; they shall speak with new tongues" (Mark 16:17). "Behold, I and the children whom the Lord hath given me are for *signs and for wonders* in Israel from the Lord of hosts, which dwelleth in mount Zion" (Isa. 8:18).

Today, we see believers running after signs when their *lives* should be the signs and wonders to a dying generation starving from a lack of God's power. We run after all kinds of phenomenons without testing the spirits as the apostle John told us, "Beloved, believe not every spirit, but try the spirits whether they are of God: because many false prophets are gone out into the world" (1 John 4:1). The Good News Bible says it this way, "My dear friends, do not believe all who claim to have the Spirit, but test them to find out if the spirit they have comes from God." We must have a genuine move of the Holy Spirit, which always glorifies Christ and never a man. Jesus said, "And I, if I be lifted up from the earth, will draw all men unto Me" (John 12:32). It is not going to be our natural talents and strengths that will put the devil on the run. It will be the anointing. "For by strength shall no man prevail" (1 Sam. 2:9).

Power is your birthright! Are you ready to step into your birthright? Doctor Luke wrote, "And Jesus returned in the power of the Spirit into Galilee" (Luke 4:14). I pray that you will have the same testimony. "Thy people shall be willing in the day of Thy *power*" (Ps. 110:3). Once you know how to access the anointing, your life will never be the same. "The Spirit of the Lord will come upon thee, and thou shalt prophesy with them, and *shalt be turned into another man*" (1 Sam. 10:6).

Chapter 2

YOU ARE ANOINTED

Many believers who hear the word *anointing* or *anointed* immediately think of someone like Oral Roberts, Benny Hinn, Kenneth Copeland, Kathryn Kuhlman, or some famous minister. The reality of the Scripture, however, is that you are also anointed. Yes, you read that correctly. *You are anointed!* Both the apostles John and Paul reveal this tremendous truth in their epistles.

"Now He which stablisheth us with you in Christ, and hath *anointed us*, is God" (2 Cor. 1:21). Notice it says, "God *has* anointed you." It is in the past tense, meaning it is a done deal. This is God's perspective. This is how you look through God's eyes. As far as He is concerned, He has anointed you. From now on, this is the way you must see yourself. You are anointed! But you say, "Brother Glenn, I don't feel like I'm anointed." To that I would say, your feelings have nothing to do with it. You are anointed whether you feel like you are or not simply because God said so in His Word.

Consider these scriptures:

- "But the anointing which ye have received of Him abideth in you" (1 John 2:27).

- "Now He which stablisheth us with you in Christ, and hath *anointed* us, is God" (2 Cor. 1:21).

- "But we have this treasure in earthen vessels, that the excellency of the power may be of God, and not of us" (2 Cor. 4:7).

The word *abideth* means that which is resident in you. The apostle John means, "You have received an anointing and it is resident or indwells you." Then the apostle Paul explained, "You have treasure within you, and it is God who has anointed you." What does that mean? Paul is saying that you don't have to run helter-skelter, looking for the anointing. It is already within you. You have spiritual power in your physical body. In the Old Testament people had to go *to* the anointing, but in the New Testament the anointing *comes into* you and abides in your body. The apostle Paul emphasized this when he wrote, "What? Know ye not that your body is the temple of the Holy Ghost which is in you, which ye have of God, and ye are not your own?" (1 Cor. 6:19). Once again, you are anointed whether you feel like it or not simply because God said so in his Word.

A Closer Scrutiny

The Word of God describes three major types of anointing:

1. *Believer's anointing*—This is for you and every born-again, blood-bought child of God.

2. *Ministerial anointing*—This was for prophets, priests, and kings in the Old Testament and the "fivefold" ministry gifts in the New Testament.

3. *Corporate anointing*—This is for the Church Body as a whole. It includes the local assemblies and believers gathered together.

We have focused on the ministerial anointing. We have been tremendously blessed in past and present generations by great men and women of God who shook the world. But as the apostle John revealed, the believer's anointing is resident in every Christian. While we are thankful for awesome, anointed ministers, it is time to realize that we are also carriers of the anointing. We read in First John 2:20, "But ye have an unction from the Holy One, and ye know all things." Then in First John 2:27, it says, "But the anointing which ye have received of Him abideth in you."

You have an unction, and you have received an anointing! The word *unction* means ointment that has been rubbed in. Notice it did not say, "The preacher has received a special anointing and not you." *Au contraire,* you are the one being talked about in these verses. The apostle John was addressing all believers. That includes you! So from now on, see yourself as anointed. Let this be your confession, "I have received an anointing from God, and it abides in me. I am anointed."

The believer's anointing is also known as the leper's anointing. In fact there is a threefold anointing that is poured out upon the New Testament believer through the New Birth: "But ye are a chosen generation, a royal priesthood, an holy nation, a peculiar people; that ye should shew forth the praises of Him who hath called you out of darkness into His marvelous light" (1 Pet. 2:9).

The Leper's Anointing

In the Old Testament, the anointing was solely for the consecration of a priest, prophet, or king and the cleansing of a leper. As you may be aware, leprosy was an incurable disease in olden days. This is a perfect type and shadow of sin from which man could not redeem himself. "And the rest of the oil that is in the priest's hand he shall put upon the head of him that is to be cleansed, to make an atonement for him before the Lord" (Lev. 14:29). Through the cross of Calvary, Jesus' redemptive blood delivered us from the curse of spiritual leprosy. Thank God!

According to Levitical ceremonial law, the leper was required to stay outside the camp. This is a picture of an unredeemed man who is far from God and can in no way be part of the life of God. The priest would then go outside the camp, taking sacrificial blood and sprinkle the leper seven times, and he would be cleansed. After this, when the leper would come into the camp, the priest would take the same blood that he sprinkled him with earlier and apply it to the cleansed leper's ear, thumb, toe, and over his head. This was followed by the application of oil. The blood application is a type of the blood of Christ, while the application of the oil is symbolic of the anointing of the Holy Spirit upon a life. The new-birth experience is an anointing that every blood-bought believer possesses! Every born-again believer has experienced the leper's anointing, which represents that he has been redeemed, cleansed from sin, and received salvation.

The Priestly Anointing

"And thou shalt put upon Aaron the holy garments, and anoint him, and sanctify him; *that he may minister unto Me in the priest's office*" (Exod. 40:13). With the new birth also comes the priestly anointing to minister to God. What an awesome privilege we have to enter into the presence of the Lord. Prior to the Christ's death on the cross, only the high priest could enter into His presence once a year. But listen to this:

> And from Jesus Christ, who is the faithful witness, and the first begotten of the dead, and the Prince of the kings of the earth. Unto Him that loved us, and washed us from our sins in His own blood, and hath made us kings and priests unto God and His Father; to Him be glory and dominion for ever and ever. Amen (Revelation 1:5-6).

The Kingly Anointing

In the Old Testament, the priest ministered unto God, but kings went into battle with their enemies, repossessing what had been taken from them, protecting their people, and restoring peace to the land. But in the New Testament, all believers are kings and priests. "But ye are a chosen generation, a royal priesthood, an holy nation, a peculiar people; that ye should shew forth the praises of Him who hath called you out of darkness into His marvelous light" (1 Pet. 2:9). "Unto him that loved us, and washed us from our sins in His own blood, and hath made us kings and priests unto God and His Father; to Him be glory and dominion for ever and ever. Amen" (Rev. 1:6).

As kings we are to use what Jesus has made available to us to dominate satan, his cohorts, and life's situations. Kings rule and reign. As kings, we will also make a decree, for the Word declares, "where the word of a king is, there is power" (Eccles. 8:4).

Death reigned over us, but through the abundance of grace poured out upon us by Jesus our Messiah, we can now reign in this life and the life to come. Through the new birth, Jesus gave us authority and power. "For if by one man's offence death reigned by one; much more they which receive abundance of grace and of the gift of righteousness shall reign in life by One, Jesus Christ" (Rom. 5:17).

Anointing Within and Anointing Upon

The apostle John said, "The anointing abides within you" (1 John 2:27). Usually when the Bible talks about the anointing, it refers to the anointing coming upon an individual. Paul said we have "this treasure in earthen vessels" (2 Cor. 4:7). In the Old Testament the treasure came *upon* an earthen vessel, but in the New Covenant, the treasure is *in* the earthen vessel. Every time the Spirit came upon someone, it was in order to accomplish a supernatural feat, as in the lives of David, Elijah, Samson, and Jesus.

When the Spirit came upon Samson, he was able to lift the gates of the city and walk thirty miles. Now Samson did not look like Arnold Schwarzenegger or Mr. Universe. He was a regular guy. The difference in his life was the anointing of God. When the anointing came upon Samson, he could tear a lion into pieces with his bare hands. When the anointing came upon Elijah, he was able to outrun the king's best horse. In the Old Testament, the anointing was always associated with a supernatural manifestation. Praise the Lord!

Another thing you should note in the Old Testament is that when you read, "the hand of the Lord was on" or "...upon," this is synonymous with "the Spirit came upon." In the Old Testament, the people did not experientially know about the Spirit *within*, only the Spirit *upon*.

Samson

Read these scriptures from the Old Testament referring to Samson:

And the Spirit of the Lord came mightily upon him, and he rent him as he would have rent a kid, and he had nothing in his hand (Judges 14:6).

And the Spirit of the Lord came upon him, and he went down to Ashkelon, and slew thirty men of them, and took their spoil, and gave change of garments unto them which expounded the riddle. And his anger was kindled, and he went up to his father's house (Judges 14:19).

And when he came unto Lehi, the Philistines shouted against him: and the Spirit of the Lord came mightily upon him, and the cords that were upon his arms became as flax that was burnt with fire, and his bands loosed from off his hands (Judges 15:14).

Elijah

Now read this scripture concerning Elijah:

And the hand of the Lord was on Elijah; and he girded up his loins, and ran before Ahab to the entrance of Jezreel (1 Kings 18:46).

New Testament

In contrast, notice what the New Testament says:

"But the anointing which ye have received of Him abideth in you" (1 John 2:27).

"But we have this treasure in earthen vessels, that the excellency of the power may be of God, and not of us" (2 Corinthians 4:7).

The Scriptures clearly reveal to us a dual working of the Holy Spirit. It is the Spirit within and the Spirit upon. Each has different workings or operations. There is the treasure of the anointing *within* and the treasure of the anointing *upon*. What is the difference? First of all, as previously mentioned, in the Old Testament they did not have the indwelling of the

Spirit because the Old Testament believers were not born again. Their spirits were not new creatures recreated by God. "Therefore if any man be in Christ, he is a new creature: old things are passed away; behold, all things are become new" (2 Cor. 5:17).

Being indwelt by the Spirit is a New Testament marvel. That is why Jesus said, "I tell you the truth, it is better for you that I go away. When I go away, I will send the Helper to you. If I do not go away, the Helper will not come" (John: 16:7 NCV). The same Holy Spirit that was in Jesus when He walked the earth is in us. Paul emphasized this reality in his letter to the Roman church, "But if the Spirit of Him that raised up Jesus from the dead dwell in you, He that raised up Christ from the dead shall also quicken your mortal bodies by His Spirit that dwelleth in you" (Rom. 8:11).

> Being indwelt by the Spirit
> is a New Testament marvel.

When we receive Jesus as our Savior, the Holy Spirit comes in and imparts eternal life into our spirits and we become His temple or a vessel of His glory. Thank God that the Holy Ghost is in us. He is with us, for us, and in us. That is shouting ground! In the Old Testament, the Holy Spirit could only come upon people, and when He did it was for a manifestation of a supernatural act.

To really emphasize this in your thinking, consider this:

- The anointing *within* is the indwelling or abiding presence of God in your life. The anointing *upon* is the manifested presence of God on your life.

- The anointing *within* is the authority of God in your life. The anointing *upon* is the display of God's power in your life.

- The anointing *within* is passive anointing, meaning resident or inhabitant. The anointing *upon* is active, meaning expressive.

Another way to fix it in your mind, would be:

Anointing *within*	Anointing *upon*
Resident	Seasonal
Inward	Outward
Invisible	Visible
Internal	External
Personal benefit	Benefit others
Salvation	Service
Knower	Enabler
Presence	Power
Abiding presence	Manifested presence
Well	River
Inward witness	Outward witness
Boldness to enter God's presence	Boldness to invade satan's presence

Whether it is the believer's anointing or ministerial or corporate, the purpose of the anointing is to destroy, upset, and uproot the works of satan in the lives of people. It is imperative for you to know and realize that you can increase and grow in the anointing. The Word declares, "Jesus grew in wisdom and stature" (Luke 2:52 NIV). That doesn't just mean physically. The more you grow in wisdom, the more you will grow in stature. The word *stature* also means somebody's standing or level of achievement. The more you grow and increase in the anointing, the more you will increase in standing and achievements. "But the anointing which ye have received of him abideth in you" (1 John 2:27).

God wants you to grow in His anointing. There's no doubt about that! You can do great exploits as you grow in a great anointing.

Chapter 3

DEFINING
THE ANOINTING

When I was a young Christian, I often heard preachers and church members proclaiming the importance of the anointing, but no one ever explained to me what the anointing was. I wanted to know how to get and increase the anointing in my life. But all I heard from other Christians were the words, "The anointing breaks the yoke!" The Scriptures bear that out. "And it shall come to pass in that day, that his burden shall be taken away from off thy shoulder, and his yoke from off thy neck, and the yoke shall be destroyed because of the anointing" (Isa. 10:27).

So then I knew two things about the anointing. It destroys yokes, and it gives us goose bumps in a church service. Needless to say, this was a very limited understanding of the issue. But many believers still don't know much more than that. I kept asking, which brought even more answers that answered nothing. I was told by many well-meaning folks, "We know what we feel, but we just can't describe it." Some said, "We know the anointing is present, but we can't verbalize it in a way you would understand." Some thought the anointing was emotionalism. Although it affects your emotions, it isn't emotionalism. The anointing is not a shout, and it isn't total silence. All these can be effects of the anointing, but they are not the anointing. Finally, I had to search the Scriptures for myself in order to gain some understanding.

Let us get a proper understanding of the anointing from the Scriptures. Don't forget that the apostle Paul called the anointing the treasure hidden in earthen vessels. The following are a few definitions. They are not in any order of importance, as they are all important.

The Anointing Is the Burden-Removing, Yoke-Destroying Power of God

The prophet Isaiah gives us a good and the most effective meaning of the anointing. In Isaiah 10:27 it says, "And it shall come to pass in that day, that his burden shall be taken away from off thy shoulder, and his yoke from off thy neck, and the yoke shall be destroyed because of the anointing." The Hebrew word here for *anointing* is *shemen*, which means oil fat. There are many Hebrew words for the word anointing that we will look at later. But here in Isaiah we learn that the anointing lifts the enemy's burdens from our shoulders and destroys his yokes.

How do you know when the anointing is present? When your yokes are destroyed and your burdens are removed. How do you know when a church is anointed? When you attend that church, your yokes are destroyed and your burdens are removed. How do you know when a preacher is anointed? It is not because he spits on you or speaks eloquently in perfect English, but because when you come in contact with him, your yokes are destroyed and your burdens are removed.

I want you to note that it says the anointing will destroy the yoke. Many times people misquote this verse by saying, "The anointing breaks the yoke." In fact, it does much more. It destroys and obliterates it. Praise God!

The Anointing Is the Presence of the Lord

Isaiah 10:27 says, "And it shall come to pass in that day, that his burden shall be taken away from off thy shoulder, and his yoke from off thy neck, and the yoke shall putrify at the presence of the oil"

(Douay-Rheims Bible). The anointing has always referred to the presence of God, regardless of whether it is passive or active. Look at this part of the verse: "the yoke shall putrify at the presence of the oil." Whenever the presence of the Lord shows up, something marvelous and extraordinary happens.

The Bible declares, "In thy presence is fullness of joy" (Ps. 16:11). When God's manifested presence comes into a place, every devil must flee. As we saw with the children of Israel, every obstacle must fall away before you. Why did the Red Sea get out of the way of God's people? What provoked it? See what the psalmist says in Psalm 114:1-8:

> *When Israel went out of Egypt, the house of Jacob from a people of strange language; Judah was his sanctuary, and Israel his dominion. The sea saw it, and fled: Jordan was driven back. The mountains skipped like rams, and the little hills like lambs. What ailed thee, O thou sea, that thou fleddest? thou Jordan, that thou wast driven back? Ye mountains, that ye skipped like rams; and ye little hills, like lambs? Tremble, thou earth, at the presence of the Lord, at the presence of the God of Jacob; which turned the rock into a standing water, the flint into a fountain of waters.*

Now connect this psalm with Psalm 77:16-18:

> *The waters saw Thee, O God, the waters saw Thee; they were afraid: the depths also were troubled. The clouds poured out water: the skies sent out a sound: Thine arrows also went abroad. The voice of Thy thunder was in the heaven: the lightnings lightened the world: the earth trembled and shook.*

Therefore, the anointing is the presence of the Lord that will cause your problems to skip out of the way.

The Anointing Is a Divine Enablement and Facilitation

Zechariah 4:6-7 says:

> *Then he answered and spake unto me, saying, this is the word of the Lord unto Zerubbabel, saying, Not by might, nor by power, but by My spirit, saith the Lord of hosts. Who art thou,*

O great mountain? Before Zerubbabel thou shalt become a plain: and he shall bring forth the headstone thereof with shoutings, crying, Grace, grace unto it.

That's what the anointing is. It is an enabler. The anointing should not be confused with natural talent. It is the Holy Spirit of God enabling you to do what you cannot do in your natural power. It is the ability of God meeting your inability to obtain biblical results. You cannot heal the sick, but the anointing in and upon you will destroy sickness from people's lives.

The anointing is the ability of God meeting your inability to obtain biblical results.

The Anointing Is the Power of God

Acts 10:38 says: "God anointed Jesus of Nazareth with the Holy Ghost and with power; who went about doing good and healing all that were oppressed of the devil." Acts 1:8 says, "But ye shall receive power after that the Holy Ghost is come upon you." The word *power* comes from the Greek word *dunamis*. It is from this word that we get our English word *dynamite*, which means explosive power. The anointing is God's explosive power to destroy the works of satan in the lives of His people. Kathryn Kulman, a powerfully anointed woman, once declared, "If you find the power of God, you have found heaven's treasure."

Jesus was anointed for a specific purpose. The apostle John reveals that purpose to us in First John 3:8: "For this purpose the Son of God was manifested, that He might destroy the works of the devil." The word *destroy* in the Greek text is the word *luo*, and it literally means the following:

- To loose any person or thing tied or fastened
- To loose one bound, to unbind
- To release from bonds

- To set free one bound up (swathed in bandages) or bound with chains (a prisoner)
- To discharge from prison, let go
- To loosen, undo, or dissolve, anything bound, tied, or compacted together
- To dismiss, break up
- To annul, subvert
- To do away with, to deprive of authority, whether by precept or act
- To declare unlawful
- To loose what is compacted or built together, to break up, demolish, destroy
- To dissolve something coherent into parts, to destroy
- To overthrow, to do away with

The anointing is the power of God's presence to loosen the demonic stronghold of any shape or form over one's life. As we read in Acts 1:8 and Acts 10:38, we cannot separate the Holy Spirit from His power. Therefore the anointing is the power of the Holy Spirit coming upon you to destroy the works of satan. We know satan's works are sickness and disease, poverty, failure, and every negative in the world.

> The anointing is the power of God's presence to loosen the demonic stronghold.

The Anointing Is a Demonstration of the Supernatural Works of God

We read in First John 3:8, "For this purpose the Son of God was manifested that He might destroy the works of the devil." John 9:4 says, "I must work *the works of Him* that sent me, while it is day." And John 10:32 says, "Jesus answered them, Many good works have I shewed you from *my Father*." God's works are good works that benefit mankind, whereas satan's works are destructive to humankind. The anointing is the physical manifestation of the works of God against the oppressive works of satan. Here is the evidence of the work of God: "God anointed Jesus of Nazareth with the Holy Ghost and power: who went about *doing good, and healing all those who were oppressed of the devil;* for God was with Him" (Acts 10:38). Always remember:

- Sickness is the work of the devil but healing is the work of God. Jesus healed all manner of diseases and all who came to Him.
- Oppression is the work of the devil but deliverance is the work of God.
- Depression is the work of satan but joy unspeakable, full of glory, is the work of God.
- Poverty is the work of satan but prosperity is the work of God.

The Anointing Is the Impartation of God's Grace and a Crown

The impartation of God's ability into our lives to do His work is called the anointing. It is the supernatural ability imparted by God to a yielded vessel to perform His assignment. It is God gracing you to fulfill your life's calling. It is your enthronement and place of crowning. Leviticus 21:12 says, "For the crown of the anointing oil of His God is upon Him: I am the Lord." Then in Second Samuel 5:3-5, we read:

All the elders of Israel came to the king to Hebron; and king David made a league with them in Hebron before the Lord: and they anointed David king over Israel. David was thirty years old when he began to reign, and he reigned forty years. In Hebron he reigned over Judah seven years and six months: and in Jerusalem he reigned thirty and three years over all Israel and Judah.

30

The Anointing Is the End of a Cycle of Frustration

Many of God's people and ministers are frustrated because they have not seen their vision fulfilled and, therefore, cannot perform the task God has assigned them. Some have received a mandate to take the city but do not know how to go about this monumental task. See what the preacher stated: "The labour of the foolish wearieth every one of them, because he knoweth not how to go to the city" (Eccles. 10:15).

Our ability to perform is limited in the natural, but when God's anointing comes upon us, the supernatural ability of God enhances our performance. Supernatural ability caused many to perform tasks beyond human and physical capabilities. Elijah ran faster than the king's horse and killed four hundred prophets of Baal. Samson picked up heavy weights, tore a lion to pieces, and destroyed all of Israel's enemies. Philip ran faster than a speeding bullet when he was translated from one city to the next. And a young man named David slew a giant named Goliath. These feats would have been impossible for them in the natural, but the anointing of God enhanced their performances and made the impossible possible.

The Anointing Is the Hand of God Removing Satan's Handiwork

Satan's hands bring destruction, fear, and failure, while the anointing is God's hand removing the hands of satan from our lives. Whenever the Bible talks about the hand of God, it is always referring to magnificent demonstrations of His power to deliver. So the anointing brings great deliverance. Judges 14:6 says, "And the Spirit of the Lord came mightily upon him, and he rent him as he would have rent a kid, *and he had nothing in his hand.*"

The Anointing Is the Help of the Holy Spirit

Romans 8:26 says, *"Likewise the Spirit also helpeth our infirmities: for we know not what we should pray for as we ought: but the Spirit itself maketh intercession for us with groanings which cannot be uttered."* Do you realize the very first time the Spirit of God is mentioned in the Scripture, it says, "And the Spirit of God moved upon the face of the waters" (Gen. 1:2). The anointing will help you in your shortcomings and weaknesses. The Holy Ghost's anointing will be with you when you face life-threatening diseases and help you win against them. The word *helpeth* is the Greek word *sunantilambanomai*. It means to take a hold together with and against. That is the help of the anointing. It comes to take a hold of you together and against your problem.

The Anointing Is the Producer of Outstanding Results

The anointing is the ability of God meeting your inability to obtain biblical results. You cannot obtain biblical results in your own strength and will power. Your flesh cannot generate the supernatural. The apostle Paul made these two emphatic statements, the first in Romans 7:18, "For I know that in me (that is, in my flesh), dwelleth no good thing." The second is in Philippians 3:3, "For we are the circumcision, which worship God in the spirit, and rejoice in Christ Jesus, and have no confidence in the flesh."

The Anointing Is Divine Backing

The anointing is also God backing you up. When God backs you up, you become unstoppable. When God stands with you, who can stand against you? You cannot fail when God backs you up. See God's word to Joshua: "There shall not any man be able to stand before thee all the days of thy life: as I was with Moses, so I will be with thee: I will not fail thee, nor forsake thee" (Josh. 1:5).

The Anointing Means You Are "Under the Influence"

We have all heard this term used, and it is always in connection with something negative. We hear of people under the influence of alcohol. Almost everyone has heard of a person being under the influence of an evil spirit. We understand that this means something is behind a person causing him to do what he is doing. To be under the influence of God will cause you to do what you cannot do naturally. "And be not drunk with wine, wherein is excess; but be filled with the Spirit" (Eph. 5:18).

The Anointing *Is* the Treasure and Storehouse of God

We read in 2 Corinthians 4:7, "But we have this *treasure* in earthen vessels, that the excellency of the power may be of God, and not of us." The word *treasure* literally means "storehouse." The anointing is treasure inside of you. There is a storehouse of God's great blessings inside of you. When you tap into the anointing, you are tapping into God's reserves that belong to you. If that is true, then your life is not empty, but it is full of the riches of God.

The Anointing *Is* the Shout That Brings the Walls Down and Destroys the Enemy

Consider these stories:

So the people shouted when the priests blew with the trumpets: and it came to pass, when the people heard the sound of the trumpet, and the people shouted with a great shout, that the wall fell down flat, so that the people went up into the city, every man straight before him, and they took the city (Joshua 6:20).

And he divided the three hundred men into three companies, and he put a trumpet in every man's hand, with empty pitchers, and lamps within the pitchers. And he said unto them, Look on me, and do likewise: and, behold, when I come to the outside of the camp, it shall be that, as I do, so shall ye do. When I blow with a trumpet, I and all that are with me, then blow ye the trumpets also on every side of all the camp, and say, The sword of the Lord, and of Gideon. So Gideon, and the hundred men that were with him, came unto the outside of the camp in the beginning of the middle watch; and they had but newly set the watch: and they blew the trumpets, and brake the pitchers that were in their hands. And the three companies blew the trumpets, and brake the pitchers, and held the lamps in their left hands, and the trumpets in their right hands to blow withal: and they cried, The sword of the Lord, and of Gideon. And they stood every man in his place round about the camp: and all the host ran, and cried, and fled. And the three hundred blew the trumpets, and the Lord set every man's

33

sword against his fellow, even throughout all the host: and the host fled to Bethshittah in Zererath, and to the border of Abelmeholah, unto Tabbath (Judges 7:16-22).

He hath not beheld iniquity in Jacob, neither hath He seen perverseness in Israel: the Lord his God is with him, and the shout of a king is among them (Numbers 23:21).

The Anointing Is a Double Portion

The term *double portion* was used to refer to the blessing of the son, but it means much more than that. The anointing is also connected to the double portion as we see in the life of Elisha.

The *double-portion* anointing is also:

- ❧ The *former* and *latter* rain
- ❧ Baptized with the *Holy Ghost* and *fire*
- ❧ The Spirit *upon* and Spirit *within*
- ❧ *Kings* and *priests*

After two days will He revive us: in the third day He will raise us up, and we shall live in His sight. Then shall we know if we follow on to know the Lord: His going forth is prepared as the morning; and He shall come to us as the rain, the latter and former rain unto the earth (Hosea 6:2-3).

Be glad then, ye children of Zion, and rejoice in the Lord your God: for He hath given you the former rain moderately, and He will cause to come down for you the rain, the former rain, and the latter rain in the first month (Joel 2:23).

Be patent therefore, brethren, unto the coming of the Lord. Behold, the husbandman waiteth for the precious fruit of the earth, and hath long patience for it, until He receive the early and latter rain (James 5:7).

I indeed baptize you with water unto repentance: but He that cometh after me is mightier than I, whose shoes I am not worthy to bear: He shall baptize you with the Holy Ghost, and with fire: Whose fan is in His hand, and he will thoroughly purge

His floor, and gather His wheat into the garner; but He will burn up the chaff with unquenchable fire (Matthew 3:11-12).

The Anointing Is Divine Protection and Establishment

Consider these powerful truths from the psalmist:

I have found David my servant; with My holy oil have I anointed him: With whom My hand shall be established: Mine arm also shall strengthen him. The enemy shall not exact upon him; nor the son of wickedness afflict him. And I will beat down his foes before his face, and plague them that hate him (Psalm 89:20-23).

He suffered no man to do them wrong: yea, He reproved kings for their sakes; saying, Touch not Mine anointed, and do My prophets no harm (Psalm 105:14-15).

The Anointing Is the Seven Spirits of God

In the three scriptures that follow, we find a unique word reference to the seven Spirits of God. In Revelation 1:4, we read, "John, to the churches which are in Asia: Grace be unto you, and peace, from Him which is, and which was, and which is to come; and from the seven Spirits which are before His throne." Revelation 4:5 says, "And out of the throne proceeded lightnings and thunderings and voices: and there were seven lamps of fire burning before the throne, which are the seven Spirits of God." Then we read in Revelation 5:6, "And I beheld, and lo, in the midst of the throne and of the four beasts, and in the midst of the elders, stood a Lamb as it had been slain, having seven horns, and seven eyes, which are the seven Spirits of God sent forth into all the earth."

The Bible, and especially the Book of Revelation, uses the number seven to refer to perfection and completion. The Greek word translated as *seven* is *hepta*, which also means "sevenfold." The term "seven Spirits" does not mean there are seven Holy Spirits, nor does it mean that the Holy Spirit has six brothers. Instead, it refers to the perfect and complete Holy Spirit. It also indicates the sevenfold characteristics and

ministries of the Holy Spirit. There is one Holy Spirit with seven different manifestations or characteristics. What are they?

Isaiah 11:1-3 says:

> *And there shall come forth a rod out of the stem of Jesse, and a
> Branch shall grow out of his roots: And the spirit of the Lord
> shall rest upon him, the spirit of wisdom and understanding,
> the spirit of counsel and might, the spirit of knowledge and of
> the fear of the Lord; and shall make him of quick understand-
> ing in the fear of the Lord.*

Revelation 5:5 tells us, "And one of the elders saith unto me,
Weep not: behold, the Lion of the tribe of Juda, the Root of David,
hath prevailed to open the book, and to loose the seven seals thereof."
Then we read in Revelation 22:16, "I Jesus have sent Mine angel to
testify unto you these things in the churches. I am the root and the
offspring of David, and the bright and morning star."

The "Rod out of the stem of Jesse" and the "Root of David" are
both Jesus and the "Branch that grows out of the root" is the Church.
Then we see seven glorious manifestations that rested upon Jesus and
now rest upon you and me—the Church, His Body:

1. The Spirit of the Lord
2. The Spirit of Wisdom
3. The Spirit of Understanding
4. The Spirit of Counsel
5. The Spirit of Power
6. The Spirit of Knowledge
7. The Spirit of the Fear of the Lord

Different Hebrew and Greek Words for "Anointing"

Mashach

One of the Hebrew words for *anoint* is *mashach*. It means to smear
with oil, to rub with oil in order to release fragrance, to consecrate for
a sacred purpose. It is from this Hebrew word that we get the word

Messiah, which means the anointed one. Imagine that your hands are cupped together holding oil, then you open them to allow the oil to flow down over a person. Being anointed indicates the substance and touch of God are upon the person

Dashen

As seen in Psalm 23:5, "Thou anointest my head with oil; my cup runneth over," and Ecclesiastes 9:8, "Let thy garments be always white; and let thy head lack no ointment," *dashen* means to be fat and prosperous. When God's anointing hits your head, your cup will never be empty. Understand that God wants you to be anointed from the top of your head to the tip of your toes.

Balal

Psalm 92:10 says, "But my horn shalt Thou exalt like the horn of an unicorn: I shall be anointed with fresh oil." The *balal* anointing gives supernatural promotion and strength. I especially love one rendition of this verse: "But You have promoted me, so that I am like a powerful buffalo: I am anointed with fresh oil." I like that! A powerful buffalo. Another translation uses the term "wild ox" and another one "unicorn." Can you see the picture?

When you're anointed, it doesn't mean that you're a softie pushover for the devil. Instead you become the devil's worst nightmare. You are not some tame ox that can be burdened down or yoked with infirmities and calamities. A wild ox is capable of overcoming every form of burden and the heaviest of yokes. Because it has not been tamed, it does not know it is supposed to carry heavy loads for man. A wild ox will rebel against all form of yokes and burdens. This is what happens to you when you have a fresh *balal* anointing on your life. You will rebel against everything the devil tries to put on your life.

Deuteronomy 33:24-25 says, "And of Asher he said, Let Asher be blessed with children; let him be acceptable to his brethren, and *let him dip his foot in oil. Thy shoes shall be iron and brass;* and as thy days, so shall thy strength be."

Glory be to God! The devil's head is going to be flatter as you dip your foot in oil and stomp his head with it. Be like Jesus and crush the devil's head under your feet. You can crush cancer! You can crush generational curses! You can crush any infirmity.

There are two words in the Greek that are translated "anointing." *Aleipho* simply means anointing. "And they cast out many devils, and anointed with oil many that were sick, and healed them" (Mark 6:13). *Chrio* means to rub and that which is consecrated to holy office. This Greek word was used to describe the anointing upon Jesus. "God anointed Jesus of Nazareth with the Holy Ghost and with power: who went about doing good, and healing all that were oppressed of the devil; for God was with Him" (Acts 10:38).

The difference between *aleipho* and *chrio* can be lost as both are translated as *anoint* in our English versions. *Aleipho* is really referring to the common use of oil. It is a general term used for *an anointing* of any kind, even physical refreshment after washing, while *chrio* refers to the sacred act and commissioning. W.E. Vine's *Expository Dictionary of New Testament Words* states, "Among the Greeks it was used in other senses than the ceremonial, but in the Scriptures it is not found in connection with secular matters."

Symbols of the Anointing

ᜄ **Oil**

He poured of the anointing oil upon Aaron's head, and anointed him, to sanctify him (Leviticus 8:12).

Then Samuel took the horn of oil, and anointed him in the midst of his brethren: and the Spirit of the Lord came upon David from that day forward. So Samuel rose up, and went to Ramah (1 Samuel 16:13).

Then shalt thou take the anointing oil, and pour it upon his head, and anoint him (Exodus 29:7).

Is any sick among you? let him call for the elders of the church; and let them pray over him, anointing him with oil in the name of the Lord (James 5:14).

Thou anointest my head with oil; my cup runneth over (Psalm 23:5).

❦ Water

I will pour water upon him that is thirsty, and floods upon the dry ground: I will pour My spirit upon thy seed, and My blessing upon thine offspring (Isaiah 44:3).

He shewed me a pure river of water of life, clear as crystal, proceeding out of the throne of God and of the Lamb (Revelation 22:1).

He said unto me, It is done. I am Alpha and Omega, the beginning and the end. I will give unto him that is athirst of the fountain of the water of life freely (Revelation 21:6).

The Spirit and the bride say, Come. And let him that heareth say, Come. And let him that is athirst come. And whosoever will, let him take the water of life freely (Revelation 22:17).

❦ River

Afterward he measured a thousand; and it was a river that I could not pass over: for the waters were risen, waters to swim in, a river that could not be passed over (Ezekiel 47:5).

In the last day, that great day of the feast, Jesus stood and cried, saying, If any man thirst, let him come unto Me, and drink. He that believeth on Me, as the scripture hath said, out of his belly shall flow rivers of living water. (But this spake He of the Spirit, which they that believe on Him should receive: for the Holy Ghost was not yet given; because that Jesus was not yet glorified) (John 7:37-39).

And he shewed me a pure river of water of life, clear as crystal, proceeding out of the throne of God and of the Lamb (Revelation 22:1).

❦ Fire

John answered, saying unto them all, I indeed baptize you with water; but One mightier than I cometh, the latchet of whose shoes I am not worthy to unloose: He shall baptize you with the Holy Ghost and with fire (Luke 3:16).

And when the day of Pentecost was fully come, they were all with one accord in one place. And suddenly there came a sound from heaven as of a rushing mighty wind, and it filled all the house where they were sitting. And there appeared unto them cloven tongues like as of fire, and it sat upon each of them. And they were all filled with the Holy Ghost, and began to speak with other tongues, as the Spirit gave them utterance (Acts 2:1-4).

Then the fire of the Lord fell, and consumed the burnt sacrifice, and the wood, and the stones, and the dust, and licked up the water that was in the trench (1 Kings 18:38).

❧ Rain

After two days will He revive us: in the third day He will raise us up, and we shall live in His sight. Then shall we know, if we follow on to know the Lord: His going forth is prepared as the morning; and He shall come to us as the rain, the latter and former rain unto the earth (Hosea 6:2-3).

Be glad then, ye children of Zion, and rejoice in the Lord your God: for He hath given you the former rain moderately, and He will cause to come down for you the rain, the former rain, and the latter rain in the first month (Joel 2:23).

Be patient therefore, brethren, unto the coming of the Lord. Behold, the husbandman waiteth for the precious fruit of the earth, and hath long patience for it, until He receive the early and latter rain (James 5:7).

❧ Well

Whosoever drinketh of the water that I shall give him shall never thirst; but the water that I shall give him shall be in him a well of water springing up into everlasting life (John 4:14).

Therefore with joy shall ye draw water out of the wells of salvation (Isaiah 12:3).

✐ Hand of the Lord

I have found David My servant; with My holy oil have I anointed him: With whom My hand shall be established: Mine arm also shall strengthen him. The enemy shall not exact upon him; nor the son of wickedness afflict him. And I will beat down his foes before his face, and plague them that hate him (Psalm 89:20-23).

The word of the Lord came expressly unto Ezekiel the priest, the son of Buzi, in the land of the Chaldeans by the river Chebar; and the hand of the Lord was there upon him (Ezekiel 1:3).

The hand of the Lord was upon me, and carried me out in the spirit of the Lord, and set me down in the midst of the valley which was full of bones (Ezekiel 37:1).

✐ Wind

Then said He unto me, Prophesy unto the wind, prophesy, son of man, and say to the wind, Thus saith the Lord God; Come from the four winds, O breath, and breathe upon these slain, that they may live. So I prophesied as He commanded me, and the breath came into them, and they lived, and stood up upon their feet, an exceeding great army (Ezekiel 37:9-10).

The wind bloweth where it listeth, and thou hearest the sound thereof, but canst not tell whence it cometh, and whither it goeth: so is every one that is born of the Spirit (John 3:8).

When the day of Pentecost was fully come, they were all with one accord in one place. And suddenly there came a sound from heaven as of a rushing mighty wind, and it filled all the house where they were sitting. And there appeared unto them cloven tongues like as of fire, and it sat upon each of them. And they were all filled with the Holy Ghost, and began to speak with other tongues, as the Spirit gave them utterance (Acts 2:1-4).

✐ Dew

Behold, how good and how pleasant it is for brethren to dwell together in unity! It is like the precious ointment upon the head, that ran down upon the beard, even Aaron's beard: that went down to the skirts of his garments; as the dew of Hermon, and as the dew that descended upon the mountains of Zion: for there the Lord commanded the blessing, even life for evermore (Psalm 133:1-3).

When the dew fell upon the camp in the night, the manna fell upon it (Numbers 11:9).

My doctrine shall drop as the rain, my speech shall distil as the dew, as the small rain upon the tender herb, and as the showers upon the grass (Deuteronomy 32:2).

I will be like the dew to Israel; he will blossom like a lily. Like a cedar of Lebanon he will send down his roots (Hosea 14:5 NIV).

Cloud

They will tell it to the inhabitants of this land: for they have heard that Thou Lord art among this people, that Thou Lord art seen face to face, and that Thy cloud standeth over them, and that Thou goest before them, by day time in a pillar of a cloud, and in a pillar of fire by night (Numbers 14:14).

Yet Thou in Thy manifold mercies forsookest them not in the wilderness: the pillar of the cloud departed not from them by day, to lead them in the way; neither the pillar of fire by night, to shew them light, and the way wherein they should go (Nehemiah 9:19).

It came even to pass, as the trumpeters and singers were as one, to make one sound to be heard in praising and thanking the Lord; and when they lifted up their voice with the trumpets and cymbals and instruments of musick, and praised the Lord, saying, For He is good; for His mercy endureth for ever: that then the house was filled with a cloud, even the house of the Lord; so that the priests could not stand to minister by reason of the cloud: for the glory of the Lord had filled the house of God (2 Chronicles 5:13-14).

⤫ Power

Jesus said, Somebody hath touched Me: for I perceive that virtue is gone out of Me (Luke 8:46).

But Jesus said, someone did touch Me, for I perceived that power had gone forth from Me (Luke 8:46 ASV).

But Jesus told him, Someone deliberately touched Me, for I felt healing power go out from Me (Luke 8:46 NLT).

But ye shall receive power, after that the Holy Ghost is come upon you: and ye shall be witnesses unto Me both in Jerusalem, and in all Judaea, and in Samaria, and unto the uttermost part of the earth (Acts 1:8).

⤫ Wine

I will be as the dew unto Israel: he shall grow as the lily, and cast forth his roots as Lebanon. His branches shall spread, and his beauty shall be as the olive tree, and his smell as Lebanon. They that dwell under his shadow shall return; they shall revive as the corn, and grow as the vine: the scent thereof shall be as the wine of Lebanon (Hosea 14:5-7).

These men are full of new wine (Acts 2:13).

Chapter 4

THE ANOINTING IN EVERY BOOK OF THE BIBLE

The anointing is visible all throughout the Bible, just as Jesus is the central theme throughout all the Scriptures. So let us look and meditate upon these wonderful truths.

In *Genesis*, the anointing is—

> The Spirit of God moving upon the face of the waters and darkness
>
> Noah's dove and rainbow
>
> Abraham and Sarah's visitations
>
> Jacob's ladder
>
> Joseph's dreams and interpretations

In *Exodus*, the anointing is—

> Moses' basket
>
> The rod of signs and wonders
>
> The pillar of cloud by day and pillar of fire by night
>
> The power of God's deliverance

In *Leviticus*, the anointing is—

    Holy oil for the priest

In *Numbers*, the anointing is—

    Aaron's rod that budded

    The reverser of Balaam's curse

    The shout of the king in our midst

In *Deuteronomy*, the anointing is—

    Manna and dew coming down from Heaven

    Allegiance to the covenant

In *Joshua*, the anointing is—

    The splitting of the River Jordan

    The trumpet blast that made Jericho's walls fall down

    The sun and moon standing still

In *Judges*, the anointing is—

    Samson's spirit of might

    Ehud's left hand and dagger

    Deborah's song

    Jael's nail

    Jeptha's restoration to leadership

In *Ruth*, the anointing is—

    The favor and wealth of Boaz

In *First Samuel*, the anointing is—

    Samuel's horn of oil

    David's harp

    David's slingshot

In *Second Samuel*, the anointing is—

    Conviction and the one who touches the heart

    The touch of God transferred from David to his men that turned them from being discontented, distressed, and in debt to become David's mighty men

In *First Kings*, the anointing is—

    Elijah's speed

    Elijah's strength

    Fire from above

    Elijah's mantle

In *Second Kings*, the anointing is—

    The double portion

    The floating axe head

    The Spirit of repentance upon Josiah to destroy idolatry

In *First Chronicles*, the anointing is—

    Gold and silver for the work of God

In *Second Chronicles*, the anointing is—

    The glory cloud that filled the house

In *Ezra*, the anointing is—

    The rebuilder of the temple and city

    The stirrer of the hearts of the people

In *Nehemiah*, the anointing is—

    The comforter to rebuild the broken wall

    The joy of the Lord

In *Esther*, the anointing is—

    The scepter of favor and deliverance

In *Job*, the anointing is—

    The restoration of the godly from the charge and accusations of satan

    The double recompense

    The turning of captivity

In *Psalms*, the anointing is—

    The oil of gladness

    Fresh oil

The horn of the unicorn

In *Proverbs*, the anointing is—

The Spirit of knowledge and wisdom

In *Ecclesiastes*, the anointing is—

The right time and season

In *Song of Solomon*, the anointing is—

Love that cannot be extinguished

In *Isaiah*, the anointing is—

The coal of fire that touched the lips

The train that filled the temple

Prophecies of the coming of the suffering servant,
the Messiah

Hezekiah's life increased

In *Jeremiah*, the anointing is—

The fire shut up in the bones

The Word of the Lord to a rebellious people

In *Lamentations*, the anointing is—

The burden of intercession

New mercies every morning

In *Ezekiel*, the anointing is—

Visions from God

The four winds

The hand of God

The promise of the New Jerusalem

In *Daniel*, the anointing is—

Dreams from God

Daniel's excellence

Daniel's deliverance from the lions' den

Perseverance for the promise

In *Hosea*, the anointing is—

> The drawing of backsliders back to the Lord
>
> The ransoming of God's people from the power of the grave
>
> The betrothal of the Lord in faith to His people
>
> The faithfulness of God

In *Joel*, the anointing is—

> The Spirit poured upon all flesh
>
> The former and latter rain

In *Amos*, the anointing is—

> The call of God that equips a nobody to stand before kings
>
> The power of agreement to walk together

In *Obadiah*, the anointing is—

> Deliverance upon Mount Zion
>
> The house of Jacob possessing its possession
>
> The fire and the flame burning in the house of God

In *Jonah*, the anointing is—

> Jonah's deliverance
>
> Jonah's preaching
>
> The power of conviction
>
> God's unfailing love for humanity

In *Micah*, the anointing is—

> Being filled with power and the Spirit of the Lord
>
> The destruction of witchcraft from God's people

In *Nahum*, the anointing is—

> A stronghold in the day of trouble for those that trust in God
>
> The overrunning flood and darkness that will pursue God's enemies
>
> The promise that affliction will not rise a second time

In *Habakkuk*, the anointing is—

> The writing of the vision and the instruction to run with it
>
> The brightness of light and rays of light coming out of God's hand
>
> The hiding of God's power

In *Zephaniah*, the anointing is—

> Mighty in our midst to save
>
> The gathering back again and making our name a praise in all the earth
>
> The turning of our captivity before our eyes

In *Haggai*, the anointing is—

> The building of God's house
>
> The signet ring of God's authority

In *Zechariah*, the anointing is—

> The oil flowing from the golden lampstand
>
> The plumb line
>
> The rebuking of satan
>
> The new garment of holiness

In *Malachi*, the anointing is—

> The unchanging nature of God
>
> The Sun of Righteousness rising with healing in His wings
>
> The promise of Elijah and the great and dreadful day of the Lord

In *Matthew*, the anointing is—

> The star that led the wise men to Jesus

In *Mark*, the anointing is—

> The immediate and instant power to heal the sick and cast out devils

In *Luke*, the anointing is—

> The Spirit of the Lord who was sent to preach the gospel to the poor, to heal the brokenhearted, to preach deliverance to the captives and recovering of sight to the blind, to set at liberty them that are bruised, and to preach the acceptable year of the Lord

In *John*, the anointing is—

> The Spirit of Truth
>
> The Comforter
>
> The Guide

In *Acts*, the anointing is—

> The tongues of fire
>
> Peter's shadow
>
> Paul's aprons
>
> Philip's translation

In *Romans*, the anointing is—

> The Intercessor
>
> The Spirit of life in Christ Jesus
>
> The Spirit that raised Jesus from the dead
>
> The Spirit of adoption
>
> The bruising of satan underneath our feet

In *First Corinthians,* the anointing is—

> The demonstration of the Spirit and of power
>
> The searcher of the deep things of God
>
> The nine gifts of the Spirit

In *Second Corinthians,* the anointing is—

> The strength to endure life's tough situations
>
> The down payment
>
> The treasure in earthen vessels

The Spirit that gives life

Liberty

In *Galatians*, the anointing is—

The effectual working in the lives of Peter and Paul

The working of miracles

The fruit of the Spirit

In *Ephesians*, the anointing is—

The spirit of wisdom and revelation in the knowledge of God

The equipper of the fivefold ministries of apostle, prophet, evangelist, pastor, and teacher

The strengthener with might in the inner man

In *Philippians*, the anointing is—

The supply of the Spirit

Rejoicing always in all things

In *Colossians*, the anointing is—

The fullness of the Godhead bodily

The One who made all things and holds all things together

In *First Thessalonians*, the anointing is—

The rapture of the church

Praying without ceasing

The faithfulness of God who has called you and will do it

In *Second Thessalonians*, the anointing is—

The Spirit of the Lord's mouth to consume the wicked

The recompense of trouble to them that trouble you

In *First Timothy*, the anointing is—

The gift given through prophecy and the laying on of hands of the elders

The apostolic ordination

The infallibility of the God-breathed Scripture

In *Second Timothy*, the anointing is—

>The Spirit of love, power, and a sound mind

In *Titus*, the anointing is—

>The blessed hope of Christ's glorious appearing

In *Philemon*, the anointing is—

>The sharing of our faith

In *Hebrews*, the anointing is—

>Alive and sharper than a double-edged sword
>
>The Eternal Spirit
>
>The Spirit of Grace
>
>The better name, the better priesthood, the surety of a better covenant and the blood of God above the blood of bulls and goats.

In *James*, the anointing is—

>The prayer of faith that heals the sick

In *First Peter,* the anointing is—

>The Spirit of glory
>
>The feeder of the flock of God

In *second Peter,* the anointing is—

>A surer word of prophecy
>
>Patience until the coming of the Lord

In *First John,* the anointing is—

>Love
>
>The unction in the believer to know all things
>
>A witness in the earth

In *Second John,* the anointing is—

>The enabler to walk in the truth

In *Third John,* the anointing is—

>The power to prosper and be in health

In *Jude*, the anointing is—

> The prophecy of Enoch declaring the Lord's second coming in advance
>
> Building up our most holy faith
>
> Praying in the Holy Ghost

In *Revelation*, the anointing is—

> The Second Coming of Jesus Christ the true Messiah, the King of kings and the Lord of lords

Chapter 5

GROWING IN
THE ANOINTING

As a believer or a minister, you can grow in the anointing. The more you grow in the anointing, the more fruit of victory you will taste in your life. Just as a person grows physically and mentally, you can also grow spiritually. The river of God's anointing can flow out of you. There is no need to settle for a little trickle or stream when a mighty river is available. "He that believeth on Me, as the scripture hath said, out of his belly shall flow rivers of living water. (But this spake He of the Spirit, which they that believe on Him should receive: for the Holy Ghost was not yet given; because that Jesus was not yet glorified)" (John 7:38-39).

The more you grow in the anointing, the more influence you will have on the earth, and the more you will be a threat to the kingdom of darkness. Looking at the life of King David and King Jesus, you will see growth. They went from glory to glory, and that can be duplicated in your life.

King David

Look at the progression in the life of David and see how he went from strength to strength.

ⅆ *Level 1*: David was anointed in the midst of his brethren. "Then Samuel took the horn of oil, and *anointed him in the midst of his brethren:* and the Spirit of the Lord came upon David from that day forward. So Samuel rose up, and went to Ramah" (1 Sam. 16:13).

ⅆ *Level 2*: David was anointed over the house of Judah. "Then the men of Judah came and there anointed David king over the house of Judah" (2 Sam. 2:4).

ⅆ *Level 3*: David was anointed over all Israel. In Second Samuel 5:1-4 it says:

Then came all the tribes of Israel to David unto Hebron, and spake, saying, Behold, we are thy bone and thy flesh. Also in time past, when Saul was king over us, thou wast he that leddest out and broughtest in Israel: and the Lord said to thee, Thou shalt feed My people Israel, and thou shalt be a captain over Israel. So all the elders of Israel came to the king to Hebron; and king David made a league with them in Hebron before the Lord: and they anointed David king over Israel. David was thirty years old when he began to reign, and he reigned forty years.

Second Samuel 5:10 says, "And David went on, and grew great, and the Lord God of hosts was with him."

It's clear to see that as David became older and more mature, he increased in the anointing over his life. It is also interesting to note that the word *reign* is used in conjunction with the word *anointing. You are anointed to reign in life.* What was the key to the ever-increasing anointing over David's life? Was it because God loved him more than anyone else or because God felt good one morning and zapped him with the anointing. Of course not!

Just as you take deliberate actions to grow physically by exercising your muscles, you can take deliberate steps to grow in the anointing. There is no mystery to it.

How did David grow? He grew in the anointing as he won battle after battle. Long before anybody knew of David, he was already a fighter. He announced to Goliath that he had fought a lion and a bear. You see, you will grow in the anointing as you keep winning the battles in your life. Some people think that when they are anointed, everything will be hunky-dory. Actually the more anointed you become, the more the enemy will come after you.

David kept growing in the anointing as he kept winning the good fight of faith. For example:

- David fought a lion and a bear, which represent demonic spirits.
- David fought his brethren as they were poisoned in their thinking by King Saul.
- David fought all the enemies of Israel.

As you grow in your anointing, you will find that there are battles to fight. Do not run away from the challenges and criticism that you face in ministry. Not everybody will like you. So what? This is not a popularity contest. Take their criticism, but keep pressing on. Some of your well-meaning friends will turn against you. So what? Keep moving forward. Never try to win the approval of people at the expense of the Lord's calling. Those who will grow in the anointing will have to develop a thick skin. Stop feeling sorry for yourself. Even when you make mistakes, get up, brush yourself off, and go forward. Don't ever shrink back in fear. Never allow the devil to intimidate you. Fight and grow in the anointing. David did it. Jesus did it. And you can do it, too.

Notice the progression in David's life. He was first anointed before his brothers. Samuel anointed him before his father and his brothers. Second, he was anointed over the house or tribe of Judah. Then at last, he was anointed over the whole house of Israel. When Samuel anointed him, reigning over Israel was the ultimate goal, but it took him some time to get there.

King Jesus

The Word clearly says that Jesus increased and grew in stature. This is not just referring to his height. Stature also means a person's standing and status. The more he grew in wisdom, the more he grew in status. And the more he grew in wisdom, the more he grew in the anointing. Luke 2:40,52 says, "And the child grew, and waxed strong in spirit, filled with wisdom: and the grace of God was upon Him.... And Jesus increased in wisdom and stature, and in favor with God and man."

Jesus fought and won many battles. For example:

- *Jesus fought with the devil in the wilderness and won.* "And Jesus being full of the Holy Ghost returned from Jordan, and was led by the Spirit into the wilderness, being forty days tempted of the devil" (Luke 4:1-2).

- *Jesus fought His brothers or, rather, His brothers fought Him.* "He [Jesus] came unto His own, and His own received him not" (John 1:11). "Then the Jews took up stones again to stone Him. Jesus answered them, Many good works have I shewed you from My Father; for which of those works do ye stone Me? Therefore they sought again to take Him" (John 10:31-32,39).

- *Jesus fought all the principalities and powers and won.* "But we speak the wisdom of God in a mystery, even the hidden wisdom, which God ordained before the world unto our glory; which none of the princes of this world knew: for had they known it, they would not have crucified the Lord of glory" (1 Cor. 2:7-8).

When you look at the vision that God gave to Ezekiel of waters flowing out from the temple of God and these waters becoming a great river, it becomes easier to see and understand the increase and growth in the anointing.

*Afterward he brought me again unto **the door of the house;** and, behold, waters issued out from under the threshold of the house eastward: for the forefront of the house stood toward the east, and the waters came down from under from the right side of the house, at the south side of the altar. Then brought he me out of the way of the gate northward, and led me about the way* *without unto the utter gate by the way that looketh eastward; and, behold, there ran out waters on the right side. And when the man that had the line in his hand went forth eastward, he measured a thousand cubits, and he brought me through the waters; the waters were to the ankles. Again he measured a thousand, and brought me through the waters; the waters were to the knees. Again he measured a thousand, and brought me through; the waters were to the loins. Afterward he measured a thousand; and it was a river that I could not pass over: for the waters were risen, waters to swim in, a river that could not be passed over* (Ezekiel 47:1-5).

The very first thing you must realize is that the source of the river is the temple. The river is actually coming out from the "front door" of God's house and Jesus said, "I am the door" (John 10:7). *The course of the river passes by the altar.* The Bible has a lot to say about the altar and its significance. Let's look at three important points.

1. *The altar is where the natural makes a connection with the spiritual.* We see this vividly in African and Asian nations where there are altars all over the city used to invoke gods or spirits. An altar is a place of spiritual transaction, where flesh connects with the spirit world. A church is an altar where people can meet with the supernatural God. So if a church does not believe in the supernatural, it really defeats its point as an altar.

2. *The altar is the place of sacrifice where death takes place.* All the millions of little lambs that were slaughtered to cover man's sins were placed on altars. Most importantly Calvary is the greatest altar ever erected as the Lamb of God, Jesus, offered Himself as man's substitute to take away the sins of the world.

3. *The altar is the place of prayer in total dependence upon God.* This is how spiritual transactions are made—the natural making a demand upon the supernatural on the altar of prayer.

Ezekiel saw the vision of this great the river and its benefit of life to everything it touches. In the vision Ezekiel was ushered deeper and deeper into the river. Each depth represents a level of spiritual maturity.

- *Ankle level.* This is the beginning of the Christian life. Baby Christians are not yet ready to swim.

- *Knee level.* The knee speaks of prayer. At this level, Christians are learning to pray and developing a prayer life and dependence on God's power.

- *Waist depth.* In describing the armor of God, Paul tells us to have our loins or waist girded with truth. Jesus said the Word is truth. So the waist depth is to be established in good and sound doctrines. "Stand therefore, having your loins girt about with truth" (Eph. 6:14). The Contemporary English Version says it this way, "Be ready! Let the truth be like a belt around your waist." The loin is also the reproductive area and when we are established in truth, we will be productive.

- *Swimming depth.* This is the level where the Christian becomes aware of the deeper things of God. As the Bible says, deep calls unto deep where the marvels of God are. This is the goal God has for all his children. God will never throw us into things over our heads without first preparing us. He will prepare us first. Let's jump into the river!

Chapter 6

Seven Ways: Meditation— Siphoning the Oil

As I mentioned at the beginning of the book, what you are reading is the result of an intense time of prayer. The Spirit of God spoke into my spirit and in my study of God's Word. I have found seven ways to effectively increase the anointing upon a believer's life.

Increasing in the anointing is not a haphazard event over which you have no control or say so. It is not like you wake up one day and find that God has zapped you because he was in a generous mood. There are deliberate actions you can take to build your muscles and increase your physical strength. In the same way, there are deliberate acts you can take to purposely increase the anointing which is already in and upon you. As you know, taking deliberate negative actions or sin will have a certain outcome as well. Those actions will hinder the flow of power out of your life. How much better to take positive actions that will cause the rivers of living waters to gush out of you. Jesus said, "Out of your belly shall flow rivers of living water" (John 17:38).

The writer of Hebrews boldly proclaimed, "For he that cometh to God must believe that He is, and that He is a rewarder of them that diligently seek him" (Heb. 11:6). Another rendering of this verse from The Message is, "He cares enough to respond to those who seek Him."

God responds to those who seek Him. To the degree that you seek God or seek increase in the anointing, to that degree it will be measured back to you. Jesus further said, "Seek and you shall find…. For every one that asketh receiveth; and he that seeketh findeth; and to him that knocketh it shall be opened" (Matt. 7:7-8).

My First Trip in Cote D'ivoire

The West African nation of Cote D'Ivoire was the site of my first major international missionary trip. This was in the early 1990s. The capital city, Abidjan, was the first city in mainland Africa in which I ministered the Gospel, and what a privilege that was. Since this was my first solo missionary trip, I was excited and yet apprehensive. The political climate was unstable, and I saw many things that thrilled me and some that freaked me out. It was there that I saw people putting snakes into their mouths—now you know that freaked me out! It was there that I saw the biggest lizard I had ever seen—and that thrilled me!

The churches were amazing and the people responded to the teaching of God's Word. I will never forget one evening. I was in a car returning from a service when the car suddenly came to a stop in the middle of a busy commercial road. "What happened?" I asked, and one of the protocol team in the car looked at me, bemused. I gathered he did not have a clue. Cars were flashing by us at ridiculous speeds. You have not seen crazy driving until you go to Africa. They are a law unto themselves.

I can tell you, I was not a happy camper to be stuck in a broken-down car on an African street in the middle of political turmoil. Finally the problem was discovered. The car was out of gas. The gauge was not functioning and the needle was stuck in the middle. The protocol explained in his African accent, "Sa, we are out of foowel!" This is what they call gas—fuel or petrol.

This was not good news since we were nowhere near a gas station. Then I saw the most amazing thing. The protocol man waved and stopped a car. He talked to the driver, who then opened the trunk of his car, took out a hose, and put it in his gas tank. The protocol then started sucking on it. My eyes popped out, and I asked, "What are you doing?" The protocol man looked at me and said, "Sa, dis is Afrikaa!" I will never forget this as long as I live. It marked me for life as I watched as the man siphoned the gas out of one tank and then proceeded to put the gas in a container to put in the other tank. You see there was one tank full of gas and the other tank was empty. Through the process of siphoning, gas was transferred to the other vehicle. Siphoning extracts from that which is full and fills up that which is empty. That is what meditation on the Word does!

The Anointing Is on and in the Word

Let's look at Numbers 11:6-8:

> *But now our soul is dried away: there is nothing at all, beside this manna, before our eyes. And the manna was as coriander seed, and the color thereof as the color of bdellium. And the people went about, and gathered it, and ground it in mills, or beat it in a mortar, and baked it in pans, and made cakes of it: and the taste of it was as the taste of fresh oil.*

Notice that the taste of the manna was the taste of fresh oil. Oil is symbolic of the anointing! There was a fresh anointing on the manna the people gathered every day. Fresh anointing for a fresh day! Psalm 92:10 says, "But my horn shalt Thou exalt like the horn of an unicorn: I shall be anointed with fresh oil." Then in Ecclesiastes 10:1, "Dead flies cause the ointment of the apothecary to send forth a stinking savor."

The first place to look when you want to increase in the anointing is the Bible, God's Word. Unfortunately, the Israelites grew tired of the manna that kept, fed, nourished, and protected them. They did not properly appreciate God's provision. The same can be said today. Many in the church are saying, "There is nothing at all beside this manna." They are looking for an anointing separate from the Word of God. There are Christians who say, "We do not need the Bible. We do not need doctrines. We just love Jesus." Is it possible to love Jesus without loving His Word? He is the Word! If you do not love the Word you do not love Jesus! Trying to get the supernatural without the foundation of the Word will only produce emotional Christianity, and emotions without the foundation of God's Word will eventually lead to deception!

Emotions without foundation
will eventually lead to deception.

What Is Manna?

The word *manna* simply means, "what is it?" When the people of God first came in contact with manna, they didn't know what it was. Exodus 16:15 tells us, "And when the children of Israel saw it, they said one to another, It is *manna*: for they wist not what it was." Exodus 16:31 says, "And the house of Israel called the name thereof Manna: and it was like coriander seed, white; and the taste of it was like wafers made with honey."

Moses in his books described manna as seed that the people gathered daily. Our Lord Jesus said this in Luke 8:11, "Now the parable is this: The *seed* is the word of God."

Then the apostle Peter, in what is known as his doctrine, says the same thing. "Being born again, not of corruptible *seed*, but of incorruptible, by the word of God, which liveth and abideth for ever" (1 Pet. 1:23).

Get this concept into your head and spirit: *the word is the seed.* Paul told us that whatever happened in the Old Testament serves as an example for us in the New Testament. (See 1 Cor. 10:6.)

As we read in Numbers 11:7-8, the people gathered the manna daily, ground it in mills or beat it in a mortar, baked it, and made cakes out of it. The taste was as fresh oil or fresh anointing. Since the word is the seed, you must gather the word daily and beat it in a mortar—meditate on it—and let it get into your spirit and mind.

What Is Being Pumped into You?

Reading, listening, meditating upon, dwelling on, and hearing the Word is beating the seed in the mortar or mill of your mind and spirit. Listening to teachings, attending conventions, and reading books that will educate and saturate you spiritually are also means of beating the seed in the mill of your mind and spirit. *You must understand that godly, biblical teaching is not just information but formation!* What you expose yourself to is forming you for the better or for the worst.

Most importantly, attending a church that teaches the Word of God as the first and final authority is a must. Even if that church is twenty miles away, the quality of your life is dependent upon being there. So many people make the mistake of attending a church simply because it is close to them. This is like saying, "I eat out of a trash can because it is close to me." People do not realize how important church is. It is not just about church attendance! Church quality is as important as church attendance. You see, where you go determines what grows inside you. If you're going to a church that does not believe in the power of the Word, the Name, the Blood, the Power of the Spirit, or divine healing and miracles, it is just a matter of time before you roll down the slippery bank of unbelief and failure. Do not waste your time with seeker-sensitive churches! You need to go to a church where faith, power, and unshakable confidence will grow inside you.

Bake the Cake

After it had been milled, the Israelites made cakes out of it. This is acting upon the Word that you have gathered and meditated upon. Whenever you act upon the Word of God, the supernatural will be a reality. Many do not see the supernatural hand of God in their lives due to the fact that they acknowledge or mentally agree with the Word but don't act on it. James told us to be a doer of the word and not hearers only. (See James 1:23.) The psalmist declared in Psalm 34:8, "O taste and see that the Lord is good: blessed is the man that trusteth in Him." We see it again in Psalm 119:103, "How sweet are Thy words unto my *taste*! yea, sweeter than honey to my mouth!" Finally in First

Peter 2:2-3 we read, "As newborn babes, desire the sincere milk of *the word*, that ye may grow thereby: If so be ye have *tasted* that the Lord is gracious."

The Anointing Is in the Word

Meditating and acting upon the promises is siphoning the anointing oil from the Word of God. When you are reading, meditating, and acting upon the Word, you are extracting the anointing. You will experience the miraculous and do the impossible when you act upon God's Word. You will defy natural laws of deterioration when you become a doer of the Word. The woman with the issue of blood pulled anointing from Jesus, the living Word of God, as she acted upon what she heard. (See Mark 5.) There is anointing in the Word.

 Meditating and acting upon the promises is siphoning the anointing oil from the Word.

Look at what the great patriarch Job said: "When I washed my steps with butter, and the rock poured me out rivers of oil" (Job 29:6). Then in Proverbs 30:33, he says, "surely the churning of milk bringeth forth butter."

There are rivers of anointing from the butter of God's Word. Obviously butter is made from the churning of milk. The more you stir the milk of God's Word in your mind and spirit, it gets thicker and thicker. It will produce rivers of anointing. Did you notice it says, "the rock poured me out rivers of oil"? According to the apostle Paul in his first epistle to the Corinthians, the Rock is Jesus. Rivers of oil, rivers of fresh anointing will flow from the Word of God and wash through your life as you dig into it. (See 1 Corinthians 10:4.). Now look at what the great prophet Moses said:

For the Lord's portion is His people; Jacob is the lot of His inheritance. He found him in a desert land, and in the waste howling wilderness; He led him about, He instructed him, He *kept him as the apple of His eye.... He made him ride on the high places of the earth, that he might eat the increase of the fields; and **He made him to suck honey out of the rock, and oil out of the flinty rock*** (Deuteronomy 32:9-10,13).

This same scripture in the New Living Translation says, "He let them ride over the highlands and feast on the crops of the fields. He nourished them with honey from the rock and olive oil from the stony ground." In the New Century Translation, it reads, "He gave them honey from the rocks, bringing oil from the solid rock."

There is oil in the rock of God's Word. Siphon the anointing from the Holy Scriptures. Every Scripture is loaded with the oil of God, which will cause you to ride the high places of the earth. The secret of strength is in your meditation and the application of God's Word. Make up your mind today that you will be in the Word daily. Remember these simple words:

- The Word anoints.
- The Word builds.
- The Word cleanses.
- The Word corrects.
- The Word defends.
- The Word energizes.
- The Word feeds.
- The Word gives.
- The Word heals.
- The Word inspires.
- The Word instructs.
- The Word brings joy.
- The Word keeps.
- The Word brings life.
- The Word molds.
- The Words gives peace.
- The Word revives.

- The Word upholds.
- The Word is victorious.
- The Word wins.

Chapter 7

PETITION, PRAYER LIFE, AND TONGUES

There is no way around it! If you want to grow in the anointing, it is imperative that you become a person of prayer. Jesus was a man of prayer, as was the apostle Paul and also the early church. The reason why Jesus had such a miraculous and supernatural ministry was because His life was bathed in prayer. It was His breath. Prayer is the heart of spiritual life. You will notice in between all the miracles of Jesus, His time was spent saturated in prayer.

What about the Prayer Life of Jesus?

Our ultimate example is the Lord, of course, and we are told to imitate Him. We already know that the intercession of the prophetess Hannah and Simeon saturated the birth of Jesus. Look at how Jesus entered into His own ministry. Luke 3:21 says; "Now when all the people were baptized, it came to pass, that *Jesus also being baptized, and praying, the heaven was opened.*"

Prayer Opens Up Heaven

Jesus entered His ministry by praying, and we are told that the heaven opened. Prayer opens up heaven. He did not operate His ministry under a closed heaven. How about you? James stated that when Elijah prayed, the heavens were opened and the rain descended and brought forth fruit. (See James 5:17-18.) Lack of fruit in ministry is in direct proportion to a lack of prayer. Prayerlessness is the reason for barrenness and powerlessness in ministry. There is a connection between prayer and doors opening. (See Colossians 4:2.) When you pray the heaven will open over you, your church, and your ministry.

What happened when the heaven opened? Luke 3:22 says, *"And the Holy Ghost descended in a bodily shape like a dove upon Him, and a voice came from heaven, which said, Thou art My beloved Son; in Thee I am well pleased."*

The Holy Ghost Descended in a Bodily Shape

When you pray, the heaven will open and whatever you need will descend in bodily shape. Your miracle will take physical shape and bless humanity. There was also, "a voice from heaven." When the heaven above your head is opened, you will have clear access to the voice of God.

Jesus Prayed in His Earthly Ministry

Luke 5:15-16 tells us, "But so much the more went there a fame abroad of Him: and great multitudes came together to hear, and to be healed by Him of their infirmities. And He withdrew himself into the wilderness, and prayed."

Then we read, "And it came to pass in those days, that He went out into a mountain to pray, and continued all night in prayer to God" (Luke 6:12).

Jesus Prayed in His Greatest Time of Testing

"And being in an agony He prayed more earnestly: and His sweat was as it were great drops of blood falling down to the ground" (Luke 22:44).

Jesus' Present Ministry is Prayer. He is Praying Right Now

Hebrews 7:25 says, "Wherefore He is able also to save them to the uttermost that come unto God by Him, seeing He ever liveth to make intercession for them."

The life of prayer and increase in the anointing go hand in hand. There is a direct connection between prayer and power. If you are to grow in the anointing, it is of utmost importance that you develop a strong prayer life. This is where the modern church or believer is missing it. Without prayer, the church will be just a social gathering without the presence and the power of God. If you want revival you need to pray; if you want to see signs and wonders you need to pray; if you want lives to be changed, mighty healings and deliverances, then you need to pray.

You might say, "Well, I have been praying!" But what is the evidence that you have been praying? The Bible says, "The earnest (heartfelt, continued) prayer of a righteous man makes tremendous power available [dynamic in its working]" (James 5:16 AMP).

Power is the proof that you have been praying. If you do not see any manifestation of power in your life, then something needs to change.

Malachi 3:6 says, "For I am the Lord, I do not change" (AMP). If God will not change, you need to. Many have changed theology to account for their lack of power or to excuse their shortcomings. The excuses are many, but the reason is simply lack of prayer equals lack of power.

The excuses are many
but the reason is simply
lack of prayer equals lack of power.

Second Chronicles 7:14 says, "If My people, who are called by My name, shall humble themselves, pray, seek, crave, and require of necessity My face and turn from their wicked ways, then will I hear from heaven, and forgive their sin, and heal their land" (AMP). The ball is in your court. If you are already praying, pray more. When William Seymour met with John G. Lake in a Chicago hotel room prior to the Azusa outpouring, he told Lake he had been praying five hours a day. Seymour told Lake what the Spirit said to him when he asked, "What else must I do to experience revival?" The Holy Spirit replied "Pray more!" God had led this man into a deep life of prayer, assigning five hours every day for prayer. This prayer life continued for more than three years. As he was praying one day the Holy Ghost said to him, "There are better things to be had in the spiritual life, but they must be sought out with faith and prayer."

After this instruction, William Seymour increased his prayer time to seven hours a day and continued to pray that way for two years. The rest is history. John Wesley said, "It seems God doesn't do anything unless we pray."

Acts 6:4 tells us, "But we will give ourselves continually to prayer, and to the ministry of the word." The foundational apostles knew that the secret to success was in total devotion to prayer. They knew that they could not neglect prayer. Even when they became very busy in ministry, they did not allow business to get in the way of prayer.

Today satan has, to a certain degree, removed prayer from the church, and that is why we have lost our effectiveness. Prayer meeting is the least attended service all over the world. Many church leaders rely on gimmicks and guest ministers to bring revival to their churches. Revival may come through some ministers, but when they leave, the revival may also leave. What we spend lots of money to obtain can be accessed freely in prayer.

Devote Yourself to Prayer

First Thessalonians 5:17 says, "Pray without ceasing." Colossians 4:2, "Give yourselves to prayer at all times, keeping watch with praise" (BBE). The apostle Paul toward the end of his epistle to the Thessalonians, instructed them to pray without stopping. The Living Bible says it in a way we can clearly understand, "Always keep on praying" (1 Thess. 5:17).

Prayer is an important pillar in the church, and we are told to pray constantly. Many believers know this in their heads, but they do not know it experientially in their lives. Paul, being a man of prayer, was a man of power. The very first thing we know about Paul after his conversion on the road to Damascus is, "Behold He prayeth" (Acts 9:11). He declared in his Roman epistle, "Continuing instant in prayer" (Rom. 12:12). The reality of this verse is not so in many believers, and that is why there is little manifestation of power in their lives. It is not the will of God for you to walk in little power when all of God's ability is available to you. A failure of power is a failure of prayer. Failure to pray is failure in all of life. He who does not pray is robbing himself of God's help and is placing himself in a position where he cannot help people. Prayer is the foundation of a successful Christian life. Prayer and manifestation go together.

What Are the Three Things God Openly Rewards?

In His Sermon on the Mount, Jesus told us there are three things that the Father will reward openly.

1. Giving

Take heed that ye do not your alms before men, to be seen of them: otherwise ye have no reward of your Father which is in heaven. But when thou doest alms, let not thy left hand know what thy right hand doeth: That thine alms may be in secret: and thy Father which seeth in secret Himself shall reward thee openly (Matthew 6:1,3,4).

2. Prayer

When thou prayest, thou shalt not be as the hypocrites are: for they love to pray standing in the synagogues and in the corners of the streets, that they may be seen of men. Verily I say unto you, They have their reward. But thou, when thou prayest, enter into thy closet, and when thou hast shut thy door, pray to thy Father which is in secret; and thy Father which seeth in secret shall reward thee openly (Matthew 6:5-6).

3. Fasting

Moreover when ye fast, be not, as the hypocrites, of a sad countenance: for they disfigure their faces, that they may appear unto men to fast. Verily I say unto you, They have their reward. But thou, when thou fastest, anoint thine head, and wash thy face; That thou appear not unto men to fast, but unto thy Father which is in secret: and thy Father, which seeth in secret, shall reward thee openly (Matthew 6:16-18).

I like to call "prayer, fasting, and giving" the undeniable trinity. Jesus said that our heavenly Father will openly reward us for activating these three forces in our lives. Open reward means that your friends and enemies will see it. This also means the devil will see it and there is nothing he can do about it. You need to get that into your spirit. God will openly reward you for giving, praying, and fasting. Sometimes people wonder if anything is happening when they are praying and fasting.

Some have said, "I have been giving, praying, and fasting and nothing seems to be happening." That cannot be true! Jesus cannot lie. It is impossible for Him to lie. Your heavenly Father will reward you openly. Your eyes will see the fruit of your sacrifices. These three forces will put you in a different league and open you up to a different world.

Consider Cornelius

The tenth chapter of the book of Acts is monumental in church history. This is the chapter where prophecies of old regarding the salvation of the Gentiles were fulfilled. God opened the Church to the Gentile world through Cornelius and his household.

> There was a certain man in Caesarea called Cornelius, a centurion of the band called the Italian band, a devout man, and one that feared God with all his house, which gave much alms to the people, and prayed to God always. He saw in a vision evidently about the ninth hour of the day an angel of God coming in to him, and saying unto him, Cornelius. And when he looked on him, he was afraid, and said, What is it, Lord? And he said unto him, Thy prayers and thine alms are come up for a memorial before God (Acts 10:1-3).

Now remember, Jesus specifically said our heavenly Father will openly reward prayer, giving, and fasting. We know that Cornelius was not saved except that he was a religious man. In the second verse, we see that Cornelius was a man of prayer. In fact the Scripture says, "He prayed always and gave much alms." Here is Cornelius, an unsaved gentile, who prays and gives. So far he has met two of the three requirements. What of fasting? Look what Cornelius said when Peter showed up:

*Therefore came I unto you without gainsaying, as soon as I was sent for: I ask therefore for what intent ye have sent for me? And Cornelius said, **Four days ago I was fasting until this hour;** and at the ninth hour I prayed in my house, and, behold, a man stood before me in bright clothing* (Acts 10:29-30).

Cornelius met Jesus' three requirements for open rewards. He prayed, gave alms, and fasted. Cornelius had been fasting for four days when Peter showed up at his house. Through these three powerful forces, Cornelius became the instrument of God to fulfill prophecies, and his closed world opened to angelic visitation. That which was inaccessible in his life became accessible through these three powerful keys. The door that was closed tightly was now opened as he used these three keys effectively. Can you imagine what will come through you as you invest in praying, giving, and fasting?

Make Your Mark in the Earth

Throughout the ages those who have led the Church of Jesus Christ to higher standards have had a rich and full ministry of prayer. The Lord Jesus Himself declared, "It is written, My house shall be called the house of prayer; but ye have made it a den of thieves" (Matt. 21:13). The word *house* in the literal Greek means family. Jesus has declared His house or family to be a family of prayer. "But Christ as a son over His own house; whose house are we" (Heb. 3:6).

As God's constituted family of prayer on the earth, we must pray like the saints of old did. Daniel in Babylon refused to obey the king's decree. (See Daniel 6:1-23.) The latter had decreed that no man could make any petition to any god or man for thirty days, but Daniel shut his ears to the decree that would shut him out of his prayer room. Daniel 6:10 says, "[Daniel] kneeled upon his knees three times a day ...and gave thanks before his God, as he did aforetime." Prayer is the reason Daniel could be delivered from the lions' den.

Those who have left their marks on this earth have been men and women of prayer. Abraham, the father of faith, was also a man of prayer, and angels came down from heaven to talk to him. Jacob's prayer was answered in the divine encounter he had at Peniel that resulted in a great blessing.

Samuel was given in answer to Hannah's persistent prayer. "And it came to pass, as she continued praying before the Lord, that Eli marked her mouth" (1 Sam. 1:12). Hannah who was barren and a laughing stock among her peers became fruitful because of the power of prayer.

Elijah's prayer closed up the heavens for three and half years, and he prayed again and the heavens gave rain. Rain from heaven came as a direct result of prayer. The apostle James tells us that the prophet Elijah was a man "subject to like passions as we are." Aren't you glad that those men and women who were so mighty in prayer were just like us? We are prone to think that those prophets and mighty men and women of old were somehow different than we think of ourselves. Even though they lived in different times and circumstances, they had the same passions we have.

On another occasion Elijah brought down fire on Mount Carmel. The prophets of Baal cried long and loud, but no answer came from their gods. The God of Elijah who answers by fire heard and answered his prayer. The same God is still alive today. Elijah was translated and went up to heaven, but his God still lives, and we have the same access to Him that Elijah had. We, too, have the right to go to God and ask for fire from heaven to come down and consume our enemies, to burn up our dross. Elisha prayed and life came back to a dead child. (See 2 Kings 4:32-37.)

Samson is another great example of what prayer can do. After losing his strength, he prayed. His strength came back and he obtained the greatest victory as we see in Judges 16:28-30.

> *Samson called unto the Lord, and said, O Lord God, remember me, I pray thee, and strengthen me, I pray thee, only this once, O God, that I may be at once avenged of the Philistines for my two eyes. And Samson took hold of the two middle pillars upon which the house stood, and on which it was borne up, of the one with his right hand, and of the other with his left. And Samson said, Let me die with the Philistines. And he bowed himself with all his might; and the house fell upon the lords, and upon all the*

people that were therein. So the dead which he slew at his death were more than they which he slew in his life.

Job prayed, and his captivity was turned. God gave him double for his troubles and lifted him up above the height of his former prosperity in answer to prayer. Job 42:10,12 tells the story.

The Lord turned the captivity of Job, when he prayed for his friends: also the Lord gave Job twice as much as he had before.... So the Lord blessed the latter end of Job more than his beginning: for he had fourteen thousand sheep, and six thousand camels, and a thousand yoke of oxen, and a thousand she asses.

Do You Pray in Tongues?

As a Christian, it is vitally important to develop your prayer life by developing the habit of praying in tongues. There is power in praying in tongues. There is power in the supernatural language of the Holy Spirit. The entrance to the supernatural realm is through the avenue of tongues.

Mark 16:15,17 reads, "And He said unto them, Go ye into all the world, and preach the gospel to every creature.... And these signs shall follow them that believe; In My name shall they cast out devils; *they shall speak with new tongues.*" In the Great Commission, Jesus said that one sign that will follow the New Testament believer is speaking in new tongues. The word *new* is the same Greek word that is used when Paul uses the term "new creature." Second Corinthians 5:17 says, "Therefore if any man be in Christ, he is a *new* creature: old things are passed away; behold, all things are become *new.*

The Greek word for *new* is the word *kainos* and it means:

- ෨ Something new and unheard of
- ෨ Of a new kind
- ෨ A brand-new species that never existed before

Tongues Are for Us Today

When you became a born-again believer, you became a brand-new species of being that never existed before. Likewise, "speaking in tongues" is a brand-new thing that never existed before. It was not so in the time of Abraham, Moses, Elijah, and John the Baptist. But it certainly is so after the resurrection. Paul spoke in tongues, as did the apostles Peter and John and the 120 believers in the upper room on the day of Pentecost. That is why we do not see tongues mentioned in the Old Testament. Speaking or praying in tongues was and is a new phenomenon that belongs to believers on this side of the cross and resurrection.

> Speaking or praying in tongues was and is a new phenomenon that belongs to believers on this side of the cross and resurrection. New tongues should be spoken by those of the new birth.

Some have tried to say that *new tongues* meant that there won't be any cursing in your mouth. It is true there should not be profanity in the mouth of the believer, but this is not a new thing. Other theologians have said that *tongues* is an ability given to preach the Gospel in the language of foreigners. This would mean *tongues* are old languages that already existed.

Some have even said, "Tongues is from the devil." But Acts 2:11 calls them the "wonderful works of God." If praying in tongues is evil then Paul was demon-possessed because he said, "I thank my God, I speak in tongues more than ye all" (1 Cor. 14:18). Can you see how ridiculous this is? Besides the devil does not speak or pray in tongues.

Another excuse we hear today is, "Tongues is not for us today." Then why would the apostle Paul waste his time talking about tongues in regard to the function of a church service in the fourteenth chapter of the book of Corinthians? The apostle Paul also said, "Forbid not to speak with tongues" (1 Cor. 14:39), and then he uttered these powerful words, "I would that ye all spake with tongues" (1 Cor. 14:5). You cannot pick and choose what part of Paul's writings are from God and what part are his own ideas.

Now the apostle Paul did state these words, "But to the rest speak I, not the Lord" (1 Cor. 7:12). But this was in no way a reference to tongues.

Praying and speaking in tongues is a fulfillment of Jesus' prophecy on the day of His ascension. Mark 16:15,17 says, "And He said unto them, Go ye into all the world, and preach the gospel to every creature…. And these signs shall follow them that believe; in My name shall they cast out devils; *they shall speak with new tongues.*" Paul was speaking the mind of God on the matter of tongues, therefore we must hear what he has to say and live in the light of it. Speaking and praying in other tongues is for us today.

As a believer or minister who endeavors to increase in the anointing, you have to develop the art of praying in the Spirit. "Now concerning spiritual gifts, brethren, I would not have you ignorant" (1 Cor. 12:1).

A Closer Look

In your King James Version, the word *gift* is italicized. This means it was put there at the discretion of the translators, supposedly to help us. Whenever you see a word italicized in the Authorized Version, it simply means that the particular word is not in the literal text. The above verse should literally be read as, "Now concerning spiritual, brethren, I would not have you ignorant." The twelfth chapter of Corinthians does not just deal with the gifts of the Spirit but also with ministries and the Body of Christ. The word *spiritual* is the Greek word *pneumatikos* and it means:

- Things pertaining to the Spirit
- Supernatural
- The miraculous
- Movement of the wind of God

So First Corinthians 12:1 can be rendered as:

- "Now concerning things pertaining to the Spirit, brothers, I would not have you ignorant."

- "Now concerning the supernatural, brothers, I do not want you ignorant."

- "Now concerning the miraculous, brothers, I do not want you ignorant."

- "Now concerning the movement of the wind of God, brothers, I do not want you ignorant."

The supernatural and the realm of the miraculous are for the believer. Witchcraft, psychics, tarot card readers, fortune telling, druids, wizards, witches, warlocks, and the New Age are not the inventors of and do not monopolize the supernatural. What the occult calls "supernatural" is demonic infestation. The supernatural and the miraculous are for the believer. You must realize that the twelfth to the fourteenth chapters of First Corinthians deals with several supernatural topics such as:

- Gifts of the Spirit

- Ministries

- The Body of Christ, the Church

- Love

- Diversities of tongues

- Tongues as a prayer language

- Prophecy

- Tongues and prophecy in church services

What the occult calls *supernatural* is demonic infestation.

In 1 Corinthians 12:10, Paul declares, "...to another divers kinds of tongues." The Weymouth New Testament rendering of this verse is, "*to another varieties of the gift of tongues, to another the interpretation of tongues.*" Basically there are four major varieties or kinds of tongues in the New Testament:

1. Tongues for personal edification—personal heavenly prayer language

2. Tongues for interpretation—an utterance or message in tongues

3. Tongues for intercession—groanings and standing in the gap

4. Tongues as a sign to unbelievers

Growing and increasing in the anointing will require that you spend much time praying in tongues, or what is commonly known as praying in the Spirit. I realize that "praying in the Spirit" can also be defined as prayer that is led by the Holy Spirit in your known language, but as a rule praying in the Spirit is synonymous with praying in tongues.

Let's look at the many benefits of praying in tongues. Like Paul, I thank God I speak in tongues on a daily and regular basis, thus partaking of the great multifaceted benefits it renders. Satan will do his utmost to keep you away from tongues as he knows that if you tap into this glorious power you will no longer be his victim of circumstances.

Allow me to give you a working definition of tongues as a prayer language. Tongues is supernatural utterances by the Holy Spirit in a language never learned by the person doing the speaking or praying. Tongues is the language of the supernatural realm just like French is the language of France. If you want to be effective and be understood in France then you should know how to speak French because that is what they speak in that part of the world. If we want to be effective in the supernatural realm then we have to become acquainted with the supernatural language of tongues.

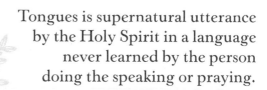

> Tongues is supernatural utterance by the Holy Spirit in a language never learned by the person doing the speaking or praying.

The Benefits of Tongues as a Private, Supernatural Prayer Language Are Many

First Corinthians 14:2 says, "For he that speaketh in an unknown tongue speaketh not unto men, but unto God: ...*howbeit in the spirit he speaketh mysteries.*" Read this scripture carefully and consider it in the points below:

1.   *Praying in tongues is the entrance into the supernatural.* There is a doorway into the realm of the spirit and it is through tongues. John said, "I was in the spirit on the Lord's day" (Rev. 1:10). No wonder Christians have no understanding of how to enter the spirit realm. Tongues unlock the spirit world. As long as satan can keep you away from tongues, he can keep you away from the miraculous. Notice the words, "howbeit it in the spirit." When you pray in tongues, you are automatically in the spirit. Paul was stating that God is in the Spirit and when we pray in tongues, we are in the Spirit where God dwells. In other words, when we start praying in tongues, we enter God's "miracle zone."

2.   *Praying in tongues is a direct line to talking to God.* First Corinthians 14:2 says, *"For he that speaketh in an unknown tongue speaketh not unto men, but unto God: ...howbeit in the spirit he speaketh mysteries."* How many people would love to have an audience with God? Literally millions! There are people all over the world doing all kinds of crazy things to get their god to hear them. Some are piercing their bodies and others are offering all kinds of sacrifices, but Paul reveals to us a direct line to the Almighty. People of all religions know that when we get an audience with God, miracles will flow. Through tongues, you and I can have direct access to God. The Word says, "no one understandeth him..." This means satan does not understand when we pray in the Spirit. He knows what you are doing but he cannot understand what you are saying. He is helpless to sabotage your prayer.

Through tongues,
you have direct
access to God.

3. *Praying in tongues is speaking divine mysteries—divinely coded secrets.* First Corinthians 14:2 says, "For he that speaketh in an unknown tongue speaketh not unto men, but unto God: ...howbeit in the spirit he speaketh mysteries." Notice the word *mysteries.* This is a loaded word that has multiple meanings, which are eye-opening. Some versions translate this word as "secrets." The Greek word is *musterion* and the meanings are:

    - Hidden things
    - Divine secrets
    - Coded language
    - Secret will or plan
    - Secret counsels that govern God in His dealing with the righteous, hidden from the ungodly and wicked men but plain to the godly
    - Knowledge withheld from ungodly, but truth revealed to the righteous
    - Images and forms

    W.E. Vine's *Expository Dictionary of New Testament Words* defines *mysteries* as "primarily that which is known to the 'mustes' meaning the initiated from *mueo,* which means to initiate into the mysteries." In the New Testament, the word *mystery* does not denote "the mysterious," as with the English word, but that which, being outside the range of unassisted natural apprehension, can be made known only by divine revelation, and is made known in a manner and at a time appointed by God, and to those only who are illumined by His Spirit. In the ordinary sense a "mystery" implies knowledge withheld; its Scriptural significance is truth revealed.

Look at First Corinthians 14:2 again. It says, "no one understandeth him." This means satan does not understand what you are saying when you pray in the Spirit. Therefore he cannot sabotage your prayer. Now look at this stated meaning, "But that which, being outside the range of unassisted natural apprehension, can be made known only by divine revelation." Therefore when you pray in tongues, secrets or plans will be made known to you.

Let's look at some other translations of First Corinthians 14:2:

- The New International Version says, "For anyone who speaks in a tongue does not speak to men but to God. Indeed, no one understands him; *he utters mysteries with his spirit.*"

- The Weymouth New Testament puts it this way, "Yet in the Spirit he is speaking secret truths."

- The Amplified Bible says, "Because in the [Holy] Spirit he utters secret truths and hidden things [not obvious to the understanding]."

  When you pray in tongues you are declaring the secrets of God, which will impart blessings and impact your life. You are prophesying your God-ordained future. By praying in the Spirit, you are making a path of blessings and power for you to walk in and enjoy.

Tongues is prophesying your God-ordained future.

4. *Praying in tongues is prophesying and praying out God's plans for your life.* Remember the word *musterion* from Point 3? It is defined as:

> ✑ Secret counsels that govern God in His dealing with the righteous, hidden from the ungodly and wicked men but plain to the godly

> ✑ Knowledge withheld from ungodly, but truth revealed to the righteous

> ✑ Secret will and plan

The anointing is strong when you are in the plan and will of God for your life. Many times people say, "I don't know what to do with my life!" or "I'm stuck!" or "I don't know where to begin!"

The plan is the wisdom of God and it is hidden *for* the believer and not *from* the believer. When you discover the plan of God then you have uncovered the wisdom of God. Paul says, "We speak the wisdom of God in a mystery" (1 Cor. 2:7). How? By praying or speaking in tongues. Solomon in his wisdom declared "wisdom is profitable to direct" (Eccles. 10:10). The plan of God is divine direction for your life, ministry, job, or any area of your life. Your next step in life and ministry will be revealed to you as you pray in the Holy Ghost. Many times even when we know the plan of God for our lives, we do not know how to implement or how to get it done. Again, that's why we must pray in the Holy Ghost to get the step-by-step plan that leads to the overall plan.

5. *Praying in tongues is to strengthen your inner man with might.* Ephesians 3:16 tells us, "That He would grant you, according to the riches of His glory, to be *strengthened with might by His Spirit in the inner man.*"

The Weymouth New Testament words it like this, "To grant you—in accordance with the wealth of His glorious perfections—*to be strengthened by His Spirit with power penetrating to your inmost being.*"

To *strengthen* means to make stronger. It also means to increase in strength and force. According to the apostle Paul, when you pray in tongues, you are strengthening or fortifying your spirit man with might. Obviously he would know more about the might of tongues as he declared to the Corinthian saints that he prayed in tongues more than them all. The word *might* is the Greek word *dunamis* and it means miracle power and explosive power. The more you pray in the spirit, the more you are increasing in spiritual force on the inside of you. The more you pray in tongues, the more explosive power and miraculous power are growing inside of you. How can you be depressed when the strength of God is within you?

The more you pray in the spirit, the more you are increasing in spiritual force on the inside of you.

6.   *Praying in tongues is home improvement and a source of spiritual edification.* Let's see how different versions render First Corinthians 14:4.

   ✺   The King James Version says, "He that speaketh in an unknown tongue edifieth himself."

   ✺   The Amplified Bible puts it like this, "...edifies and improves himself."

   ✺   The Weymouth New Testament says, "He who speaks in an unknown tongue does good to himself."

   ✺   The Good News Bible says, "Those who speak in strange tongues help only themselves."

Paul was encouraging the Corinthian church to keep praying and worshiping in tongues as a means of spiritual edification. Other versions of the Bible use the words *improves, does good, builds,* and *help themselves* to define "edification." How many of us could use some improvements right now? Tongues will improve and build you *up* in a *down* world. In fact we can safely say that tongues is *"doing home improvement."*

The word *edify* is the Greek word *oikodomeo*, which is a compound of two words: *oiko* meaning house and *domeo* meaning *to* build. When you put these two words together, it means to build a house. This word *edify* also means to charge up like you would charge a dead battery. This verse could be literally translated as, "He that speaks or prays in unknown tongues builds his house and charges himself up with spiritual current."

Have you ever felt drained and physically worn out? I know I have! Since I travel extensively to minister worldwide, many times I cross time zones and spend long hours in planes and airports. When I get to my destination, I am often physically drained. But I thank God for the ability to charge my body with spiritual energy through the avenue of tongues. This simple habit of praying in tongues has helped me again and again.

7. *Praying in tongues builds and stimulates your faith.* The King James Version of Jude 1:20 says, "But ye, beloved, building up yourselves on your most holy faith, praying in the Holy Ghost." Now let's look at that verse in the Amplified Bible, "But you, beloved, build yourselves up [founded] on your most holy faith [make progress, rise like an edifice higher and higher], praying in the Holy Spirit."

In this tiny epistle Jude warns of a time of great apostasy in the last days where right would be considered wrong and vice versa. These will be tough times! You do not need to be a rocket scientist to realize that we are living in these days of apostasy.

What you need in these tough times is strong and stimulated faith. Jude tells us that when we pray in the Holy Ghost, we are building and stimulating our world-overcoming faith. Praying in tongues is a faith booster. As you pray in tongues, you will rise higher and higher in a "down" world.

The Amplified Bible aptly translates this verse, "Build yourselves up [founded] on your most holy faith [make progress, rise like an edifice higher and higher], praying in the Holy Spirit." Notice it says "make progress." The world system under satan's influence is designed to hinder your progress in every sense of the word, but as you keep praying in tongues, your progress will become unstoppable and undeniable by your worst enemies.

> The more you pray in tongues,
> the more your progress
> will be unstoppable and
> undeniable by your enemies.

8. *Praying in tongues is giving praise and thanksgiving well unto God.* Let's read First Corinthians 14:15-17:

What is it then? I will pray with the spirit, and I will pray with the understanding also: I will sing with the spirit, and I will sing with the understanding also. Else when thou shalt bless with the spirit, how shall he that occupieth the room of the unlearned say Amen at thy giving of thanks, seeing he understandeth not what thou sayest? **For thou verily givest thanks well.**

Praying in tongues is good for you because it is another way of praising and blessing the Lord. When you release "tongues," you are releasing praise and thanksgiving to God. Paul says, *"For thou verily giveth thanks well,"* meaning this is bonafide praise. It is singing with grace in your heart.

Colossians 3:16 says, "Let the word of Christ dwell in you richly in all wisdom; teaching and admonishing one another in psalms and hymns and *spiritual songs,* singing with grace in your hearts to the Lord." The term "spiritual songs" is not a reference to gospel music, although that is included. This refers to songs from your spirit, the tongues of praise and thanksgiving that flow from your heart and through your mouth. I guarantee you that there is not one ounce of unbelief in tongues. When you are speaking or singing in tongues, there is no fear, doubt, unbelief, panic, or depression attached to it.

There is not one ounce of unbelief in praying in tongues.

9.   *Praying in tongues is praying in line with the divine will of God.*

Likewise the Spirit also helpeth our infirmities: for we know not what we should pray for as we ought: but the Spirit itself maketh intercession for us with groanings which cannot be uttered. And He that searcheth the hearts knoweth what is the mind of the Spirit, because He maketh intercession for the saints according to the will of God. And we know that all things work together for good to them that love God, to them who are the called according to His purpose (Romans 8:26-28).

In the eighth chapter of his Roman epistle, Paul gave us a very important insight into praying in tongues and its function in the spirit world. The Holy Spirit is our helper, intercessor, and comforter. He is here to help us in every area of our lives and particularly in prayer. Effective prayer has to be done according to the will of God and by faith. God does not answer and listen to unbelief. Always remember that prayer does not change God. It changes things, and it changes you. God is unchangeable. He answers our prayers, which are anchored in faith and according to His divine word.

Malachi 3:6 says, "For I am the Lord, I change not." As our helper, the Holy Spirit helps us to pray. The Greek word Paul used is *sunantilambanomai,* and it means taking hold together with and against. Of course this verse is referring to tongues because Paul says, "the Spirit itself maketh intercession for us with groanings which cannot be uttered." Groanings in the Bible does not mean moaning or complaining. It always alludes to prayer and intercession. You can see that in the Hebrew people in their moment of distress, and Jesus at the grave of Lazarus. (See Exodus 2:23-25 and John 11:33,38.) The word *groaning* here can also be translated as "that which cannot be uttered in articulate speech." Articulate speech would be English or your natural mother tongue. So we understand that "groaning" is talking about praying in tongues.

Many times we do not know exactly how we are to approach a situation in prayer, but thank God the Holy Spirit inside us comes to our aid as we pray in tongues. He comes and takes hold of us together against the problem. Side by side we stand against the enemy to remove him. There is no hope for the devil!

When you do not know what to say in prayer, the Holy Spirit knows exactly what to say, and it is always in line with God's will. You cannot fail with the Holy Spirit involved in your prayer life.

10. *Praying in tongues enables all things to work for your good.* Romans 8:27-28 says, "…because *He maketh intercession for the saints according to the will of God. And we know that all things work together for good to them that love God, to them who are the called according to His purpose.*"

   "All things work together for good" is an expression that many Christians have used to put a nice face on a bad situation. Some have used it in death, accidents, and other disappointing situations. This verse was not given by the inspiration of the Holy Spirit to excuse failures. This verse belongs to the tongue-talker. It is when you pray in tongues that all things will work for your good. Notice it says something is working for your good. Praying and interceding in tongues is working on your behalf to bring good to your life.

11. *Praying in tongues aids us in being God-inside minded.* Look at John 14:17: "Even the Spirit of truth; whom the

world cannot receive, because it seeth Him not, neither knoweth Him: but ye know Him; for He dwelleth with you, and shall be in you." Praying in tongues will be of great benefit to you because it is a constant reminder of the presence and power of the indwelling Holy Spirit. Continuous praying and worshiping in tongues will help you to be consciously aware of the reality of the indwelling Spirit. This realization will cause you to rely more on His ability rather than yours. His power is more effective than all human abilities and talents.

This is the word of the Lord unto Zerubbabel, saying, Not by might, nor by power, but by My spirit, saith the Lord of hosts (Zechariah 4:6).

For ye have not received the spirit of bondage again to fear; but ye have received the Spirit of adoption, whereby we cry, Abba, Father. The Spirit itself beareth witness with our spirit, that we are the children of God: And if children, then heirs; heirs of God, and joint-heirs with Christ (Romans 8:15-17).

As you keep praying in tongues it enables you to be consciously aware of the fact that you are a child of God, a joint heir with Jesus, and that the Holy Spirit indwells you.

12. *Praying in tongues magnifies God.* Acts 10:45-46 tells us, "And they of the circumcision which believed were astonished, as many as came with Peter, because that on the Gentiles also was poured out the gift of the Holy Ghost. For they heard them speak with tongues, and magnify God.

Apart from meaning *praise* and *thanksgiving to God, magnify* means to increase in size and capacity. When you are praying in tongues, God is getting bigger and bigger on the inside of you. The bigger God gets inside of you, the smaller the devil will be.

13. *Praying in tongues gives spiritual refreshing and rest.* Praying in tongues is good for you because it refreshes and

gives spiritual rest. "For with stammering lips and another tongue will he speak to this people. To whom He said, This is the rest wherewith ye may cause the weary to rest; and this is the refreshing" (Isa. 28:11-12).

Tongues will give you rest in the midst of warfare. We all know that we are in a fight, and if we are not cautious we can become battle-weary. Thank God we can always be refreshed and find rest as we release our prayer language. Peter, in the book of Acts says it this way, "…times of refreshing shall come from the presence of the Lord" (Acts 3:19).

This is how Paul kept himself strong, refreshed, and on the cutting edge, even though all hell was assigned against him. The man constantly prayed in tongues.

14. *Praying in tongues helps you to enter the world of the gifts of the Spirit.* The nine gifts of the Spirit are for us today. They give believers the supernatural edge we need to operate in the world. As we tap in the power of praying in tongues, it will open us up to the gifts.

15. *Praying in tongues is fine-tuning your spirit man to be sensitive and hear the voice of God.* The more we pray in tongues, the more our spirits becomes sensitive to the Holy Spirit. We adjust our spiritual tuner by praying in other tongues. Pay attention to the ideas, concepts, and insights that flow to your mind from your spirit as you pray in tongues. This is God giving you keys for your victory. Through tongues God communicates to you the steps to take to secure your victory on the earth. Tongues is not just you talking to God, but it's Him talking to you, giving you insights and keys to your problems.

Many people blast in tongues like bullets from a machine gun and then jump up and go. Take time to listen to what the Holy Spirit is saying. That is what happened to John on the Isle of Patmos, where he was sent to suffer and die by his enemies. Satan could not have anticipated what happened next. Isaiah 28:11 says, "For with stammering lips and another tongue will he speak to this people." Now let's read John's account:

I was in the Spirit on the Lord's day, and heard behind me a great voice, as of a trumpet, Saying, I am Alpha and Omega, the first and the last: and, what thou seest, write in a book, and send it unto the seven churches which are in Asia; unto Ephesus, and unto Smyrna, and unto Pergamos, and unto Thyatira, and unto Sardis, and unto Philadelphia, and unto Laodicea. And I turned to see the voice that spake with me (Revelation 1:10-12).

John was not on vacation in Patmos, he had some serious trouble and needed God to deliver him. Notice what he said, *"I was in the Spirit."* The apostle Paul has already told us that when we pray in tongues we are in the Spirit. (See 1 Corinthians 14:2.) John accessed the realm of the Spirit by praying in tongues, and when he did he heard the voice of the Lord.

You will hear the voice of the Lord when you are in the Spirit. John said he heard His voice as a trumpet and Paul said that the trumpet prepares you for war and gets you ready to fight your enemies. One word from God will change your entire life. A word from God is worth more than ten thousand words from men. God knows something about your problem that no one else knows. He knows how to deliver you, and as you pray in tongues, he drops the answer into your spirit and the rest is victory. "In the law it is written, With men of other tongues and other lips will I speak unto this people; and yet for all that will they not hear Me, saith the Lord" (1 Cor. 14:21).

16. *Praying in tongues assists you to bring your natural tongue under control.* Praying in tongues will be beneficial to you in your endeavor to control your tongue. The book of Proverbs tells us that death and life are in

the power of the tongue. (See Proverbs 18:21.) Control your tongue and you will control your life. Praying in tongues will keep me from profane, vulgar, and obscene communication. When you develop the habit of praying in tongues, you will not have time to gossip about other people, tell dirty jokes, or be involved with any other filthy communication.

17. *Praying in tongues helps you to develop intimacy with the Holy Spirit.* Tongues are the language inspired by the Holy Spirit. There is something amazing about speaking and understanding the same language. It creates an affinity and connectivity. Imagine finding yourself in a foreign land that does not speak your mother tongue. You look and feel like a stranger and all of a sudden you hear somebody speaking your language. Your ears perk up. Language connects people. Tongues will connect you to God.

18. *Praying in tongues creates an air of privacy between you and God.* Those of us who have been blessed to be fluent in two or more languages find we can use that for exclusivity and privacy. Although I speak fluent English, my mother tongue is Creole and French. Those are the languages I spoke until my family moved to London. Even though I left Mauritius many years ago, I can still converse in French and Creole. That comes in handy when I want to say something to my brothers that I don't want others around us to understand. You see when you are praying in tongues, your heavenly language, you completely cut satan off. He would love to know what you are saying, but he doesn't have a clue. It is a private conversation between you and your heavenly Father.

19. *Praying in tongues will deepen your relationship with God.* It is difficult to deepen your relationship with someone if you speak different languages. The lack of understanding becomes a major barrier to a deep, meaningful relationship, even if you have a lot of other things in common. Speaking

God's language will enable you to deepen your relationship and fellowship with Him. Never forget, how *deep* you go with God will determine how high you will go in life. Think about these scriptures:

Acquaint now thyself with Him, and be at peace: thereby good shall come unto thee (Job 22:21).

Deep calleth unto deep... (Psalm 42:7).

They that go down to the sea in ships, that do business in great waters; these see the works of the Lord, and His wonders in the deep (Psalm 107:23-24).

20. *Praying in tongues will give you access to revelation knowledge.* Praying in tongues will cause your spirit man to tap the mind of God and receive understanding from His Word. So many believers complain that they fall asleep when they read the Bible. That is because they are not able to access the hidden treasures of the Scriptures.

We speak the wisdom of God in a mystery, even the hidden wisdom, which God ordained before the world unto our glory: Which none of the princes of this world knew: for had they known it, they would not have crucified the Lord of glory. But as it is written, Eye hath not seen, nor ear heard, neither have entered into the heart of man, the things which God hath prepared for them that love Him. But God hath revealed them unto us by His Spirit: for the Spirit searcheth all things, yea, the deep things of God. For what man knoweth the things of a man, save the spirit of man which is in him? even so the things of God knoweth no man, but the Spirit of God. Now we have received, not the spirit of the world, but the spirit which is of God; that we might know the things that are freely given to us of God (1 Corinthians 2:7-12).

Now look at Romans 8:7: "Because the carnal mind is enmity against God: for it is not subject to the law of God, neither indeed can be." Then First Corinthians 2:14,

"But the natural man receiveth not the things of the Spirit of God: for they are foolishness unto him: neither can he know them, because they are spiritually discerned."

Praying in tongues will open the Bible to you from God's perspective and not just from an intellectual level. Many theologians know the Bible only on an intellectual level and there is no power in their lives. There are great truths that are yet to be revealed, and you can access them through tongues.

Chapter 8

CONSECRATION, SANCTIFICATION, AND THE IMPORTANCE OF FASTING

Lacking in a lot of churches today is consecration, separation, and sanctification. That's why many of God's people, even ministers, are walking in powerlessness. Where lawlessness reigns, so does powerlessness. The word *sanctification* simply means to be set apart for holy use. We can see that in the life of Samson, who is a great example of power in consecration and powerlessness and shame in lawlessness.

He told her all his heart, and said unto her, There has not come a razor upon mine head; for I have been a Nazarite unto God from my mother's womb: if I be shaven, then my strength will go from me, and I shall become weak, and be like any other man (Judges 16:17).

> Where lawlessness reigns, so does powerlessness.

Samson's incredible strength and demise were directly linked to his level of consecration to the Lord. The word *Nazarite* comes from the Hebrew word *nazir*, meaning consecrated or separated. The

Nazarite's vow was voluntarily made by those who desired "to separate themselves unto the Lord" for a determined season as described in the book of Numbers.

> *The Lord said to Moses, speak to the Israelites and say to them: If a man or woman wants to make a special vow, a vow of separation to the Lord as a Nazirite, he must abstain from wine and other fermented drink and must not drink vinegar made from wine or from other fermented drink. He must not drink grape juice or eat grapes or raisins. As long as he is a Nazirite, he must not eat anything that comes from the grapevine, not even the seeds or skins. During the entire period of his vow of separation no razor may be used on his head. He must be holy until the period of his separation to the Lord is over; he must let the hair of his head grow long. Throughout the period of his separation to the Lord he must not go near a dead body. Even if his own father or mother or brother or sister dies, he must not make himself ceremonially unclean on account of them, because the symbol of his separation to God is on his head. Throughout the period of his separation he is consecrated to the Lord* (Numbers 6:1-8 NIV).

During the time of his separation and sanctification, Samson's Nazarite vow bound him to *three* absolute demands:

1. *He was to practice abstinence from drinking wine or fermented drink.* The Nazarite was not allowed to drink wine or grape juice or eat anything that came from the vine.

2. *He was forbidden to cut his hair. Samson's strength was not in his hair.* Instead, it was an outward symbol of the vow he had taken. In fact, in those days, long hair was a sign of weakness, and yet it was part of the Nazarite Vow. It demonstrates two things that Paul said. The first is "for when I am weak, then am I strong" (2 Cor. 12:10). The second is "...that the excellency of the power may be of God, and not of us" (2 Cor. 4:7). The weakness of man can only rely upon the strength of God.

3. *He was forbidden to touch a dead body.* This even included family members since death portrayed sin and the fall of

man, while the Nazarite was to typify life. *"Wherefore come out from among them, and be ye separate,* saith the Lord, and touch not the unclean thing; and I will receive you"* (2 Cor. 6:17).

God is explicitly clear about the importance of "separation from the world," especially for those in the service of His Kingdom. James 4:4 says, "Ye adulterers and adulteresses, know ye not that the friendship of the world is enmity with God? Whosoever therefore will be a friend of the world is the enemy of God."

We, the modern Church need to realize that God's standards are high, and they have not changed. *There is power in purity!* Samson kept his vow of separation until he became obsessed with Delilah, who typifies "the world." Samson's delusional love for Delilah caused him to betray his love for God. Delilah's name means "feeble," and she came from the Valley of Sorek, which means "choice wine." Wine was forbidden for Samson and thus, Delilah became his feeble point. In setting his affection on Delilah, Samson lost his anointing—and he didn't even realize it. Later Samson made excuses for what he had done, trying to justify his actions.

When we start making excuses our actions become inexcusable. The Philistines overpowered, bound, and blinded Samson. They put him in prison, and then relegated him to grinding corn like a crude beast. God has strong views about loving the world more than Him. *"Love not the world,* neither the things that are in the world. If any man love the world, the love of the Father is not in him" (1 John 2:15).

Each of us has a feeble point. However, that feeble point does not have to lead to a fall. When you partake of that which is forbidden in the name of faith, your feeble point can become your fall.

> When you fellowship with that which is forbidden under the guise of faith then your feeble point will become your fall.

Under the New Covenant, believers do not need to take the Nazarite vow, but we are still expected to be separate from the world.

Separation

Separation is an essential part in the life of the believer! It is crucial to your witness, demonstrating that you have truly been saved and changed! The separation of believers was a requirement both in the Old and New Testaments. "Wherefore *come out from among them, and be ye separate,* saith the Lord, and touch not the unclean thing; and I will receive you, and will be a Father unto you, and ye shall be My sons and daughters, saith the Lord Almighty" (2 Corinthians 6:17).

The Difference Between Justification and Sanctification

As a believer you must understand that there is a major difference between *justification* and *sanctification*. It is crucially important that you understand that difference.

- ๛ Justification. Justification is the work of God where the righteousness of God is legally imputed by grace to the sinner so that the latter is declared by God as being righteous under the Law. In Justification, righteousness, which is the nature of God, is bestowed upon the believer because of what Jesus did on the cross. He fully paid the price to satisfy the claims of "heavenly justice." This righteousness is not earned by any effort of the believer, but it is given and attributed instantaneously through accepting Christ as Savior and Perfect Substitute, resulting in eternal life. It is the gift of God.

- ๛ Sanctification. Sanctification is the work of the believer in partnership with God to produce more godly character in the life of the believer who has already been justified. Unlike justification which is instantaneous, sanctification is a process because it is not the work of God alone. To say it another way, *"Justification is what God does for us, while sanctification is what God does in us."* The justified believer must be actively involved in submitting to

God, which is the basis of sanctification. If you do not submit your life, mind, body, and actions to God by obeying His written Word then resisting sin, being more godly is highly unlikely. "Having therefore these promises, dearly beloved, let us cleanse ourselves from all filthiness of the flesh and spirit, perfecting holiness in the fear of God" (2 Cor. 7:1).

Where justification is an exterior work of God, sanctification comes from God working within us by the Holy Spirit. In other words, we contribute to sanctification through our efforts. In contrast, we do not contribute to our justification through our efforts. In sanctification God is working *in* and *with* us to be holy. "Being confident of this very thing, that He which hath begun a good work in you will perform it until the day of Jesus Christ" (Phil. 1:6).

Philippians 2:12-13 says, "Wherefore, my beloved, as ye have always obeyed, not as in my presence only, but now much more in my absence, work out your own salvation with fear and trembling. For it is God which worketh in you both to will and to do of His good pleasure." Then in First Peter 1:14-16 we read, "As obedient children, not fashioning yourselves according to the former lusts in your ignorance: But as He which hath called you is holy, so be ye holy in all manner of conversation; because it is written, 'Be ye holy; for I am holy.'" Finally, in Second Timothy 2:20-22:

> *In a great house there are not only vessels of gold and of silver, but also of wood and of earth; and some to honor, and some to dishonor. If a man therefore purge himself from these, he shall be a vessel unto honor, sanctified, and meet for the master's use, and prepared unto every good work. Flee also youthful lusts: but follow righteousness, faith, charity, peace, with them that call on the Lord out of a pure heart.*

Separated from and Separated unto

When we talk about separation, there are two aspects of separation that you, as a believer, must embrace. They are both very powerful forces that will increase the anointing upon your life. "Separated from" refers to your life of consecration and sanctification, and "separated unto" refers to your dedication to the gifting that God has placed upon your life. In this chapter, we will look at "separated from." Why is it so important to the Lord that you remain separated and distinct from the world? Why does this bring glory to His name? The wisdom of God tells us, "Turn you at my reproof: behold, I will pour out My spirit unto you, I will make known My words unto you" (Prov. 1:23).

God is not obligated to anoint you to a greater measure if you are unwilling to turn at His reproof, be sanctified, and be consecrated. You must be separated and consecrated. Of course, you will need the Lord's help to be consecrated unto Him. I am not talking about sanctification from a legalistic approach that amounts to earning God's love. He loves you no matter what. But it is to your benefit to walk a consecrated and sanctified life. "Follow peace with all men, and *holiness, without which no man shall see the Lord*" (Heb. 12:14).

Master Cusser

I was not born in an English-speaking country but rather a French-speaking island. My mother tongue is Creole and French. At the age of fourteen, my family and I moved to London, and I could barely communicate. Consequently my first month in school was a major struggle.

The first thing I learned in school was not from my teachers but from my school friends. They took great pleasure in teaching me how to cuss. Now, I did not know how to communicate but I knew how to cuss. At the age of fourteen, I became a professional cusser. I could cuss out a cat. I took great pleasure and pride in the fact that I could communicate this way.

Then one Sunday morning, I went to a Pentecostal church and got saved and born again. Thank God I was not asked to testify because out of bad habit I most likely would have cussed in thanking the Lord for saving my soul. After that Sunday, I knew I was born again, I knew heaven was my home, and I knew I loved Jesus—and yet I could not stop cussing. I struggled with cussing for months, trying everything in my power to stop. It just seemed that there were so many people who legitimately needed a few words. I would cuss and repent, cuss and repent to no end. It was driving me nuts!

Finally in exasperation I told the Lord, "I can't do this by myself. I need your help." I decided that I would go to church on Sunday morning and evening. On Monday I would go to cell group, and on Tuesday I would go to the church Bible study. Most Wednesdays I would visit other cell groups. On Friday I would go to All Night prayer meeting, and on Saturday, I would go to evangelism. After weeks of getting close to God, it suddenly dawned on me that I was no longer cussing. The truth is that the closer I got to God, the more I separated myself unto Him, the quicker sin left my life. Please do not mistake separation for isolation. God does not intend for you to live like a suffering monk or a hermit. Jesus is our example of separation, sanctification, and consecration. Yet the Lord interacted with sinners without compromising His light. So what are we to be separated from?

Satan

The world is in the lap of the wicked one. What does that mean? I'm talking about the world system. We are separated *from* this world because we are separated *unto* the things pertaining to the Kingdom. We should operate from the *Word* system, not the system of the *world*. Abraham was told "Get thee out..." (Gen. 12:1). This means we must live by the principles and statutes set forth in the Word of God. It should define our culture, paradigm, mode of operation, and way of life.

Sin

Christ paid the price for our sin on the cross of Calvary. Paul says, "Sin shall not have dominion over you" (Rom. 6:14). Get away from the sin that easily besets you. Face your weaknesses head-on and do not make excuses for them. Do not try to sweep it under the carpet. There is no carpet. Do not court the forbidden. Many feel that because we are living in the day of grace that God's perspective of sin has changed from His mosaic perspective. This is simply not the case. Sin is sin in God's eyes. The Greek word for *sin* is *hamartia*, which means to "miss the mark." Of course the mark is the Word of God.

Many believers think they can play with the things of the flesh and the world and then wonder why there is no power in their lives. Some have said, "We are under grace." But being under grace does not give us a license to sin. Being under grace does not mean we trample upon God's established principles. It's true, we do not live under the Law, that is, the ceremonial and Levitical laws, but we are still accountable to God's moral laws.

Wrong Relationships

Paul says "not unequally yoked together with unbelievers" (2 Cor. 6:14). Of course that refers to marrying an unbeliever, but it also applies to other relationships. It could be a friend or a business partner. God prohibited Israel from making alliances with other nations for defensive and economic purposes. Why? Because as God told Solomon, "They will turn away your heart [from me]" (1 Kings 11:2-4,9). *You see, your relationship reveals your heart condition.* Move away from every relationship that is moving you away from God's destiny for your life. Do not be mesmerized by wrong relationships.

Both Samson and Solomon were destroyed because of wrong alliances. The prophet Amos stated, "Can two walk together except they be agreed?" (Amos 3:3). When Jehoshaphat made a trade alliance with Israel's wicked king, Ahaziah, a prophet came to him and announced, "Because thou hast joined thyself with Ahaziah, the Lord hath broken your works" (2 Chron. 20:37). Wrong relationships will defile you whereas right relationships will deter you from doing wrong.

Your relationships
reveal your heart condition.

The Importance of Fasting

There is power in fasting. It is another crucial aspect to be considered if you want to increase in the anointing. Many believers have never tapped into the benefits and power of fasting. In early church history, fasting was considered one of the pillars of Christianity.

When the church demonstrated the power of God, fasting played a major role. You will find that both in the Old and New Testaments and throughout church history, fasting was deemed essential. It was considered to be the channel of power.

Today fasting is viewed as antiquated, a medieval relic of monks and priests. What has brought revival in former generations is now mocked by modern believers. Very few believers realize the tremendous impact fasting has in the spiritual realm. It is unfortunate that most Christians do not see the importance and validity of fasting. The Bible is clear that God's people have a mandate to fast. In fact those who have had impact in this world have been those who knew the power of fasting.

The Word of God is full of examples of people who prayed and fasted and changed their situations for the better. We know from Scriptures that Moses was a man of fasting. Elijah, Daniel, and Esther, to name just a few, also fasted. Jesus, Peter, and Paul also fasted. These were people who had power with God and therefore they had power over life's problems. There are people today who have taken the stance and declare that we do not need to fast since we are no longer under the Law. They contend that the practice was only for the early church. Looking closely at the Scriptures, we find that the Lord never did away with the principle of fasting, but man has attempted to do away with it. Some have even twisted Jesus' words in the Gospels to try to prove their point.

> *The disciples of John came to Him, saying, Why do we and the Pharisees fast often, but Your disciples do not fast? And Jesus said to them, Can the friends of the bridegroom mourn as long as the bridegroom is with them?* **But the days will come when the bridegroom will be taken away from them, and then they will fast** (Matthew 9:14-15 NKJV).

Then John 16:7 says, "Nevertheless I tell you the truth; it is expedient for you *that I go away*: for if I go not away, the Comforter will not come unto you; but if I depart, I will send Him unto you."

The answer Jesus gave is crucial for believers today. Jesus was referring to Himself as the "bridegroom" and the disciples as "the guests of the bridegroom." Actually, Jesus was saying that while He was with the disciples, it was not necessary for them to fast. However, the time would come when the bridegroom would be taken away, referring to His crucifixion, resurrection, and ascension. That would be the time for fasting. Notice the term, "then they shall fast," in the scripture from Matthew. Jesus was referring to His disciples and also to the Church, His Body. Today, physically Jesus is not with us: He is seated at the right hand of the Father. Therefore, it is now mandatory for us to fast. The Lord also declared in Matthew 6:16-18:

> *Moreover when ye fast, be not, as the hypocrites, of a sad countenance: for they disfigure their faces, that they may appear unto men to fast. Verily I say unto you, They have their reward. But thou, when thou fastest, anoint thine head, and wash thy face; That thou appear not unto men to fast, but unto thy Father which is in secret: and thy Father, which seeth in secret, shall reward thee openly.*

Jesus said *when* and not *if* you fast, implying we have to set a time to fast. Furthermore He told us that fasting is unto the Father, and there will be a reward. That should be enough incentive for a believer to realize that there is recompense when we tap into the benefits and power of fasting. The Lord Himself recognized the power of fasting. Before He began His ministry, the Holy Spirit led Him into the wilderness where He fasted for forty days. "And Jesus being full of the Holy Ghost returned from Jordan, and was led by the Spirit into the wilderness, being forty days tempted of the devil. And *in those days He did eat nothing*" (Luke 4:1-2). Then we read in Matthew 4:1-2, "Then was Jesus led up of the Spirit into the wilderness to be tempted of the devil. And when *He had fasted forty days and forty nights,* He was afterward an hungered."

During this time, Jesus fasted in order that He might be consecrated and set apart for the work His Father had given Him to do. It was a demonstration of humility to acknowledge His total submission and dependence upon God as the Source of His strength. The Word says, "Blow the trumpet in Zion, sanctify a fast" (Joel 2:15).

To *sanctify* means to set apart for holy use. Jesus set Himself apart for the work that was ahead of Him. Now if the Lord saw the importance of fasting, how much more should we? Jesus, by fasting, set an example for us to follow in His steps.

After He fasted, Jesus returned in the power and force of the Holy Spirit. "And Jesus returned in the power of the Spirit into Galilee: and there went out a fame of Him through all the region round about" (Luke 4:14). We also see that Jesus "in those days He did eat nothing" (Luke 4:2). To put it simply, *fasting means not eating*.

- In Greek the word for fasting is *nesteuo*, which means no food.

- In Hebrew the word for fasting is *tsown*, which means no food.

- In French the word for fasting is *jeuner*, which means no food.

In its simplest definition, *fasting* means to abstain from food for spiritual purposes. Now of course in many circles today, it has been said that abstaining from television or newspapers is a form of fasting. While I believe it is beneficial for us to abstain from television, I doubt that the apostles would consider these legitimate forms of fasting. The modern church, in its insistence on the gospel of comfort and ease, has expanded and changed the meaning of fasting to include more than abstaining from food. Hence fasting has lost its potency and cutting edge for many. Because many have heard about the potency of fasting but do not practice it, the church today is not wielding the same kind of raw power we saw in the early church.

A believer should fast because:

- *Fasting* is part of New Testament life.

- *Fasting* and prayer rekindles the loss of the "first love" for the Lord, which results in a more intimate relationship with Jesus Christ.

- *Fasting* allows the Holy Spirit to reveal your true spiritual condition.

- *Fasting* can transform and supercharge your prayer life into a richer and more explosive experience.

⁂ *Fasting* will produce revival in your own life and make you a channel of revival to others.

⁂ *Fasting* enables you to put your body under subjection.

Three Types of Fasting

The word *fast* literally means to shut the mouth so as to abstain from food. When you "breakfast," you partake of food and when you "fast" you abstain from food. Fasting was practiced in the Old Testament as well as the New Testament and throughout church history. It is still valid for the believer in this modern and high-tech age. There will always be those who say, "We don't have to fast; we're not under the Law." But fasting has nothing to do with the Levitical Law. It is an indication of the depth of our consecration, devotion, and dedication to God. If Jesus, the Son of God, fasted then it's only fitting that we also should fast, since we are to be imitators of Christ.

David Brainerd, the great seventeenth-century man of God who was a missionary to the American Indians in New York, New Jersey, and eastern Pennsylvania gave this instruction that you and I should heed:

"Fast as often as your health will allow and for as long as you can. For it is there that the power of God is brought to earth for effective ministry."

Another great man of God from South Africa, Andrew Murray, said,

"Fasting helps to express, to deepen, and to confirm the resolution that we are ready to sacrifice anything—to sacrifice ourselves—to attain what we seek for the kingdom of God."

One very important point I want to make is to be sure you consult with your doctor before a fast.

The Bible describes *three* major types of fasting:

1. *Normal* or *Regular Fast.* Traditionally, a regular fast means refraining from eating all food. Most people still drink water or juice during a regular fast. It is advisable to be sure you get plenty of fluids. When Jesus fasted in the

desert, the Bible says, "After fasting forty days and forty nights, He was hungry" (Matt. 4:2 NIV). This verse does not mention Jesus being thirsty.

2. *Partial Fast.* This fast is also commonly known as the "Daniel Fast." This type of fast generally asks that you omit a specific meal from your diet or refrain from certain types of foods. This is very good and suitable for those who are new to fasting, those with health issues, and the elderly. Some people have been foolish in fasting at the cost of their health, and a few have even died. Use wisdom when you fast. Remember that you are doing your fast unto the Lord and not for the eyes of people.

Daniel 10:2-3 says, "At that time I, Daniel, mourned for three weeks. I ate no choice food; no meat or wine touched my lips; and I used no lotions at all until the three weeks were over" (NIV).

In Daniel 1:12, we can clearly see that Daniel and his three friends restricted their diet to vegetables and water: "Please test your servants for ten days: Give us nothing but vegetables to eat and water to drink" (NIV).

3. *Absolute Fast.* Also known as a "Full Fast" or "Dry Fast," these fasts are complete—no food and no drink. This kind of fast can be done for one day, and the maximum would be only three days. Going longer can cause damage to your body. It is imperative for you to understand that your body can go for days without food but not without water. You need water! An absolute fast was an exceptional and unusual measure for an exceptional and unusual purpose. Dr. Luke in his treatise records that Paul went on a full fast for three days following his encounter with the Lord on the road to Damascus. Here are some examples of the Full Fast:

☞ *Paul.* Acts 9:9 says, "For three days he was blind, and did not eat or drink anything" (NIV).

⚜ *Esther.* This woman of God called for a full fast when Israel as a nation was facing persecution and extinction as recorded in Esther 4:15-16:

Then Esther sent this reply to Mordecai: Go, gather together all the Jews who are in Susa, and fast for me. Do not eat or drink for three days, night or day. I and my maids will fast as you do. When this is done, I will go to the king, even though it is against the law. And if I perish, I perish (NIV).

⚜ *Ezra.* Ezra 10:6 says:

Then Ezra rose up from before the house of God, and went into the chamber of Johanan the son of Eliashib: and when he came thither, he did eat no bread, nor drink water: for he mourned because of the transgression of them that had been carried away.

We must use wisdom when we fast. If you have never fasted before, there is no point in saying that you will go on a forty-day fast. As I already mentioned—and it bears repeating—many have not used wisdom in regard to fasting and damaged their health; for some it has even been fatal. So please don't be foolish. Think through your plan to fast thoroughly, and talk to your doctor about it. Fasting is good for your spiritual empowerment, but fast according to your ability. You give according to your ability and you minister according to your ability, so the same rule should apply to fasting. Here is a little guide of how I started my life of fasting:

⚜ 9 A.M.-6 P.M.—no food, but plenty of fluid or no food and no liquid.

⚜ 12 A.M.-3 P.M.—no food, but plenty of fluid.

⚜ 6 A.M.-6 P.M.—no food, but plenty of fluid or no food no fluid.

⚜ 6 A.M.-6 A.M. (24 hrs)—no food, but plenty of liquid.

You can customize your fast! Remember to always attach prayer to your fasting. When you fast, you are getting away from food to be with God. That is the main purpose!

Reasons for Fasting

There are many reasons why people fast. Here are some examples:

- *Esther* fasted when her nation was facing extinction, and God turned the situation around.
- *Nehemiah* fasted over the broken wall of Jerusalem.
- *Ezra* fasted for protection.
- *The people of Nineveh* fasted to avert the judgment of God.
- *Daniel* fasted for revelation.
- *The apostles* fasted for direction.
- *Anna* fasted to see the fulfillment of the Promised Seed.
- *Cornelius* fasted to receive salvation for himself and his household.
- *Joshua* fasted to expose the cause of failure.
- *Ahab* fasted to be forgiven.
- *Jehoshaphat* fasted when he was outnumbered in battle.
- *The king* fasted to shut the mouth of the lions when Daniel was thrown into the den.
- *Daniel* fasted to mourn over the sins of Israel.

The Scriptures also declare that fasting is to afflict the soul. Others fasted for spiritual power and to increase the anointing. The choice is yours!

Benefits of Fasting

While there are more benefits in fasting, the few that I have listed below should be incentive enough for you to partake in it. Take advantage of fasting! It is for you. It will change and charge your life. A bright future awaits you.

- *Fasting turns you to the Lord.* "Therefore also now, saith the Lord, turn ye even to Me with all your heart, and with fasting, and with weeping, and with mourning" (Joel 2:12). Many times in our Christian life, we are going in our own direction and not following the path of God. Fasting will put us back on the right track, which is seeking God. Fasting turns you in the right direction and that is toward God. It rekindles your love and passion for God.

❧ *Fasting humbles you.* "But as for me, when they were sick, my clothing was sackcloth: I humbled my soul with fasting" (Ps. 35:13). I have discovered that there's just as much pride in the lives of believers as there is in unbelievers. God hates pride. The apostle James said in his epistle, "God resists the proud, but gives grace to the humble" (James 4:6 NKJV). Therefore when you are walking in pride, God Himself will resist you. Fasting is a means of humbling yourself and acknowledging your total dependency upon God as your source of strength, which positions you to receive the grace and favor [preferential treatment] of God.

❧ *Fasting puts you in a position of command.* Luke 4:1,2,14 tells us:

And Jesus being full of the Holy Ghost returned from Jordan, and was led by the Spirit into the wilderness, being forty days tempted of the devil. And in those days He did eat nothing: and when they were ended, He afterward hungered. And Jesus returned in the power of the Spirit into Galilee: and there went out a fame of Him through all the region round about.

Notice after fasting Jesus returned in the power of the Spirit. The word for *power* here is *dunamis,* and it means:

❧ Explosive power

❧ Virtue

❧ Miracle power

❧ Divine strength

❧ Conquering power

How awesome! This is how your church will take the city. Not with gimmicks but with explosive power to heal the sick, cast out devils and teach with authority. Now examine what happened in the ministry of Jesus after He returned with conquering power:

- ✎ *Influence and notoriety*—"... a fame of Him through all the region round about" (Luke 4:14).

- ✎ *Taught and honored*—"And He Himself conducted [a course of] teaching in their synagogues, being recognized and honored and praised by all" (Luke 4:15 AMP).

- ✎ *Boldly revealed His mission to the world*—Luke 4:17-21 says:

  There was delivered unto Him the book of the prophet Esaias. And when He had opened the book, He found the place where it was written, The Spirit of the Lord is upon Me, because He hath anointed Me to preach the gospel to the poor; He hath sent Me to heal the brokenhearted, to preach deliverance to the captives, and recovering of sight to the blind, to set at liberty them that are bruised, to preach the acceptable year of the Lord. And He closed the book, and He gave it again to the minister, and sat down. And the eyes of all them that were in the synagogue were fastened on Him. And He began to say unto them, This day is this scripture fulfilled in your ears.

- ✎ *Authority in word and teaching*—"And came down to Capernaum, a city of Galilee, and taught them on the sabbath days. And they were astonished at His doctrine: for His word was with power" (Luke 4:31-32).

- ✎ *Made the devil cry*—Luke 4:33-36 says:

  In the synagogue there was a man, which had a spirit of an unclean devil, and cried out with a loud voice, Saying, Let us alone; what have we to do with Thee, Thou Jesus of Nazareth? art Thou come to destroy us? I know Thee who Thou art; the Holy One of God. And Jesus rebuked him, saying, Hold thy peace, and come out of him. And when the devil had thrown him in the midst, he came out of him, and hurt him not. And they were all amazed, and spake

*among themselves, saying, What a word is this! for with
authority and power He commandeth the unclean spirits,
and they come out.*

✑ *Power over diseases and devils*—Luke 4:38-41 says:

*Simon's wife's mother was taken with a great fever; and
they besought Him for her. And He stood over her, and rebuked the fever; and it left her: and immediately she arose
and ministered unto them. Now when the sun was setting,
all they that had any sick with divers diseases brought them
unto Him; and He laid his hands on every one of them,
and healed them. And devils also came out of many, crying
out, and saying, Thou art Christ the Son of God. And He
rebuking them suffered them not to speak: for they knew
that He was Christ.*

Jesus came back into his city with conquering power that
made devils cry. They could not hide from Him. Whatever devils were hiding in the synagogue could not stand
His presence when He came back. When you fast, no
devils will be able to hide in your church and ministry.

✑ *Fasting unleashes spiritual power.* "And Jesus returned in
the power of the Spirit into Galilee; and there went out a
fame of Him through all the region round about" (Luke
4:14). Fasting unleashed power for the Lord Jesus, but
the disciples were helpless when they faced the lunatic
boy. "Then came the disciples to Jesus apart, and said,
Why could we not cast him out? ...this kind goeth not
out but by prayer and fasting" (Matt. 17:19, 21).

After fasting Jesus walked in the power of the Spirit, but
many believers are quenching the Spirit due to a lack of
prayer and fasting. Power is released when you bring
your body under subjection. The more you deny your
flesh, the more you release your spirit to move in power.
It produces a force in the realm of the Spirit.

✑ *Fasting is a means of receiving direction and revelation
from God concerning His will and purpose for your life.*

After fasting, Paul and Barnabas received instruction and direction from the Holy Ghost.

Now there were in the church that was at Antioch certain prophets and teachers; as Barnabas, and Simeon that was called Niger, and Lucius of Cyrene, and Manaen, which had been brought up with Herod the Tetrarch, and Saul. As they ministered unto the Lord, and fasted, the Holy Ghost said, Separate me Barnabas and Saul for the work whereunto I have called them. And when they had fasted and prayed, and laid their hands on them, they sent them away. So they, being sent forth by the Holy Ghost, departed unto Seleucia; and from thence they sailed to Cyprus (Acts 13:1-4).

Paul and Barnabas knew the next phase of their ministry and the geographical location, too. There are many today who are jumping from one thing to another and failing because they have not taken the time to seek God's direction through prayer and fasting. After Daniel fasted—setting himself to seek the Lord—he received understanding and revelation that he did not have previously.

Fasting is another way we minister unto the Lord. We read in Acts 13:2 that "they ministered unto the Lord and fasted." Other translations use the word *worshiped* instead of ministered. So we can see that fasting is worshiping or ministering to the Lord. Fasting is worship. It is a way we can offer the quality time we generally spend eating, to the Lord in prayer. Fasting is not just for the acquisition of things but to receive an impartation from God. It is serving God as Anna the prophetess did. "And she was a widow of about fourscore and four years, which departed not from the temple, but served God with fastings and prayers night and day" (Luke 2:37).

Fasting opens a door of abundance to you. The specter of lack can be successfully attacked and destroyed when we fast. "Blow the trumpet in Zion, sanctify a fast, call a

115

solemn assembly ... Yea, the Lord will answer and say
unto His people, Behold I will send you corn, and wine,
and oil, and ye shall be satisfied therewith" (Joel
2:15,19).

Fasting shuts the door of poverty and opens the door of
blessings to you. Many of God's people are struggling
with a spirit of poverty and debt. But by tapping into the
power of fasting, they can break free from their bondages
and be a blessing to the Body of Christ. Corn in the Bible
is symbolic of prosperity and abundance. Do you recall
in the book of Genesis when there was no corn in the world
due to famine? People from all over the land had to go and
purchase corn from Joseph in Egypt. God says when you
fast there will be corn in your barn. No more lack!

Fasting increases your spiritual sharpness. It causes you to
be sensitive to the things of God. You become more aware
of spiritual things that carnal Christians don't notice.
Anna the prophetess was aware of the coming of the
Messiah, while the religious leaders were oblivious to His
appearing:

And there was one Anna, a prophetess, the daughter of
Phanuel, of the tribe of Aser: she was of a great age, and had
lived with an husband seven years from her virginity: And
she was a widow of about fourscore and four years, which departed not from the temple, but served God with fastings and
prayers night and day. And she coming in that instant gave
thanks likewise unto the Lord, and spake of Him to all them
that looked for redemption in Jerusalem (Luke 2:36-38).

Fasting stirs God to be jealous over you. The devil is in serious trouble. If anybody is going to be jealous over me,
let it be God. "Then will the Lord be jealous for his land,
and pity his people" (Joel 2:18). Webster's threefold definition of the word jealous:

• Intolerant of rivalry or unfaithfulness

- Hostile toward a rival or one believed to enjoy an advantage
- Vigilant in guarding a possession

The jealousy of God over you causes you to be His prize possession. He won't let anybody touch you. That's good news!

☞ *Fasting releases the protection of God.* A wall of protection will be set up around you as you fast. Satan will not be able to break through and steal your goods and family from you.

Then I proclaimed a fast there, at the river of Ahava, that we might afflict ourselves before our God, to seek of Him a right way for us, and for our little ones, and for all our substance. For I was ashamed to require of the king a band of soldiers and horsemen to help us against the enemy in the way: because we had spoken unto the king, saying, The hand of our God is upon all them for good that seek Him; but His power and His wrath is against all them that forsake Him. So we fasted and besought our God for this: and He was entreated of us (Ezra 8:21-23).

Then we departed from the river of Ahava on the twelfth day of the first month, to go unto Jerusalem: and the hand of our God was upon us, and He delivered us from the hand of the enemy, and of such as lay in wait by the way. And we came to Jerusalem, and abode there three days (Ezra 8:21-23).

Fasting protects you, your family, and your possessions. It keeps you safe on your life's journey. There is an enemy in the way and his name is satan, but when you fast you have protection. Presidents, prime ministers and government officials have soldiers as protection, yet some have tragically been assassinated. But when God is your protection, no weapon formed against you can prosper. When you are under the shadow of the Most High God, you become invisible to your enemies. In these days in which we now live, we need to cover ourselves more than ever from all angles, and fasting is certainly one more level to our defense system.

The God Kind of Fast

Is it such a fast that I have chosen? a day for a man to afflict his soul? is it to bow down his head as a bulrush, and to spread sackcloth and ashes under him? wilt thou call this a fast, and an acceptable day to the Lord? Is not this the fast that I have chosen? to loose the bands of wickedness, to undo the heavy burdens, and to let the oppressed go free, and that ye break every yoke? Is it not to deal thy bread to the hungry, and that thou bring the poor that are cast out to thy house? when thou seest the naked, that thou cover him; and that thou hide not thyself from thine own flesh? Then shall thy light break forth as the morning, and thine health shall spring forth speedily: and thy righteousness shall go before thee; the glory of the Lord shall be thy reward. Then shalt thou call, and the Lord shall answer; thou shalt cry, and He shall say, Here I am. If thou take away from the midst of thee the yoke, the putting forth of the finger, and speaking vanity; and if thou draw out thy soul to the hungry, and satisfy the afflicted soul; then shall thy light rise in obscurity, and thy darkness be as the noon day: And the Lord shall guide thee continually, and satisfy thy soul in drought, and make fat thy bones: and thou shalt be like a watered garden, and like a spring of water, whose waters fail not. And they that shall be of thee shall build the old waste places: thou shalt raise up the foundations of many generations; and thou shalt be called, The repairer of the breach, The restorer of paths to dwell in. If thou turn away thy foot from the sabbath, from doing thy pleasure on my holy day; and call the sabbath a delight, the holy of the Lord, honorable; and shalt honor Him, not doing thine own ways, nor finding thine own pleasure, nor speaking thine own words: Then shalt thou delight thyself in the Lord; and I will cause thee to ride upon the high places of the earth, and feed thee with the heritage of Jacob thy father: for the mouth of the Lord hath spoken it (Isaiah 58:5-14).

Here is a list of what you can expect to happen when you tap into the fast that God honors:

- *The bands of wickedness will be loosed.* Every principality or territorial devil in your city or family will bow before you. Whatever has twisted your city, community, or family will be loosened and straightened out.

- *Heavy burdens will be undone.* No more heavy loads to carry from the devil. Fasting will break the burdens and let you or those around you walk free.

- *The oppressed will go free.* Many times as we walk around our city, a sense of helplessness overwhelms us because we know that God's power is available to deliver the oppressed. But we do not know how to bring deliverance to the people. Peter's shadow healed those oppressed of the devil. Paul's handkerchiefs drove sicknesses out of people's bodies. By the hands of the apostles were great signs and wonders done. They came into the same spot that Jesus was in, "God anointed Jesus of Nazareth with the Holy Ghost and power; who went about doing good, and healing all that were oppressed of the devil" (Acts 10:38). You can come to the same spot as Jesus and the disciples.

- *You will break every yoke.* This means you! Once you have broken through and tasted victory, you will know how to do it again and again. Sometimes we want other people to break the yokes over us but when you fast, every yoke in your life—whether they are generational, ancestral, or territorial—will be broken and obliterated.

- *Then shall your light break forth as the morning.* Hallelujah! No more dark days! They are over! There is a new day coming to your life. It will be a new day and a new season. The old season of failure and darkness is over.

- *Your health shall spring forth speedily.* Sickness and infirmities which ran rampant in your family will be destroyed.

Your body will have a fresh lease on life. Your healing will spring forth quickly.

ꙮ *Your righteousness shall go before you; the glory of the Lord shall be your reward.* Protection was provided from the front and from the back. Egypt could not creep up and destroy Israel because of the pillar of fire. In the same way, God's glory will protect you.

ꙮ *You shall call, and the Lord shall answer; you shall cry, and He shall say, "Here I am."* You will no longer struggle for answered prayer. You will no longer say, "It does not seem as if my prayer is going above the roof." God's presence will be a living experience for you.

ꙮ *Your light shall rise in obscurity, and your darkness will be as the noon day.* Your darkest time will be as the noon day sun. Oh what a thought! No more black Monday or whatever else the world goes through. When Egypt was in darkness, Goshen had light. This will be your portion.

ꙮ *The Lord shall guide you continually.* You will have the divine guidance and divine direction your need to keep you safe and on course. The prophet Isaiah said, "They thirsted not when he led them through the deserts" (Isa. 48:21). No more crumbs for you.

ꙮ *Your soul shall be satisfied in drought, and your bones made fat.* You will have total satisfaction from God. Nothing will be missing or broken in your life.

ꙮ *You shall be like a watered garden, and like a spring of water, whose waters fail not.* No more dry seasons for you. Your life will be fully irrigated.

ꙮ *They that shall be of you shall build the old waste places.* Whatever was stolen from you or broken down will be restored. God will give you total recovery in all areas of your life. God is a God of restoration, restitution, and recompense. That which did not work before will now work.

❧ *You shall raise up the foundations of many generations; and you shall be called, the repairer of the breach, the restorer of paths to dwell in.* You will repair the former generation and inspire hope for the future generation. Hope for the future generation is not the responsibility of the government but of those who know how to touch God.

❧ *Then shall you delight yourself in the Lord; and I will cause you to ride upon the high places of the earth.* Your Christianity will be sweet, and you will experience the more abundant life—the high life which God intended all along for you. You will rest in your wealthy place. Your broken days will be over.

❧ *You will be fed with the heritage of Jacob your father.* Power with God and power with man was what Jacob had.

Jacob was left alone; and there wrestled a man with him until the breaking of the day. And when he saw that he prevailed not against him, he touched the hollow of his thigh; and the hollow of Jacob's thigh was out of joint, as he wrestled with him. And he said, Let me go, for the day breaketh. And he said, I will not let thee go, except thou bless me. And he said unto him, What is thy name? And he said, Jacob. And he said, Thy name shall be called no more Jacob, but Israel: for as a prince hast thou power with **God and with men, and hast prevailed.** *And Jacob asked him, and said, Tell me, I pray thee, thy name. And he said, Wherefore is it that thou dost ask after my name? And he blessed him there* (Genesis 32:24-29).

This is your portion as you tap into the power of fasting. It will make you a prince, able to rule over life's situations. You will have power with God, power and influence with men, and power over devils. Take your place!

Chapter 9

ASSOCIATION

Your associations will determine your assimilation and impartation. Simply put, we become like those we spend time with—good or
bad. "There is desirable treasure, and oil in the dwelling of the wise,
but a foolish man squanders it" (Prov. 21:20 NKJV). Young's Literal
Translation says it this way, "A treasure to be desired, and oil, is in the
habitation of the wise, and a foolish man swalloweth it up."

In your quest to increase in the anointing, it is important to realize
that who you associate with will either make or break you. There are relationships that will sap the anointing out of your life, and there are associations that will embellish the anointing over your life. Every important
change in your life will involve other people. The associations you
choose will be a determinant in the final outcome. The Bible warns
again and again about the consequences of bad relationships and the
benefits of good ones. Psalm 1:1-2 reminds us, "Blessed is the man who
does not walk in the counsel of the wicked or stand in the way of sinners
or sit in the seat of mockers. But his delight is in the law of the Lord, and
on His law he meditates day and night" (NIVUK).

The Lord Jesus Himself was aware of His relationships and associations. He spent more time with His disciples than He did with the

Pharisees. You see, who you associate with will either defile you or deploy you. He knew when to withdraw and when to pursue. He knew who to withdraw from and who to pursue.

You must understand that there is no such thing as a neutral or accidental relationship. Every relationship you have has a spiritual dimension that will either be beneficial or detrimental.

> You see, who you association
> with will either defile you
> or deploy you.

Many believers are hungry for God and want the anointing to increase in their lives, but they overlook one important element. They are doggedly determined to stay loyal to detrimental relationships and associations. They believe they are doing this in the name of love, but really it is ignorance and a violation of scriptural principles. They feel their continued connection will bring deliverance or salvation to that person. However as we often see, it is not the good that influences the bad but the bad that corrupts the good.

God will not be mocked! He has clearly told us to separate ourselves from those who practice ungodliness, as we see in this passage:

> *If any man teach otherwise, and consent not to wholesome words, even the words of our Lord Jesus Christ, and to the doctrine which is according to godliness; he is proud, knowing nothing, but doting about questions and strifes of words, whereof cometh envy, strife, railings, evil surmisings, perverse disputings of men of corrupt minds, and destitute of the truth, supposing that gain is godliness: from such withdraw thyself* (1 Timothy 6:3-5).

Here is some food for thought in regard to associations.

☞ *Those you choose to associate with will be a determinant in whether you taste victory or defeat.* Elisha tasted the double-portion anointing after choosing to associate himself with Elijah. David's men left a place of obscurity, debt, despair, and discontentment and rose to a place of prominence after deciding to associate with him.

🙢 *Those you choose to associate with will either take you into your chosen destiny or remove you from your God-given destiny.* "Blessed is the man who does not walk in the counsel of the wicked or stand in the way of sinners or sit in the seat of mockers. But his delight is in the law of the Lord, and on His law he meditates day and night" (Ps. 1:1-2 NIVUK). You cannot possibly delight in the law of the Lord if you are walking in the counsel of the ungodly, standing in the way of sinners and sitting in the seat of the scornful.

Your actions speak louder than your words. If you walk in the counsel of the ungodly, you will incur catastrophic consequences. If you stand in the way of sinners, sooner or later what they do will become acceptable to you and you will begin to justify their ways because they have gotten inside you. Judas's friendship with the Pharisees resulted in the betrayal of His Messiah. Who you associate with will determine what you embrace and who you betray. If you sit in the seat of the scornful, bitter, and arrogant, that poison will get into your spirit and defile your life.

> Who you associate with
> will determine what you
> embrace and who you betray.

🙢 *Those you choose to associate with will determine the condition of your heart.* Solomon was infatuated with wrong relationships. Eventually his relationships turned his heart away from God.

But king Solomon loved many strange women, together with the daughter of Pharaoh, women of the Moabites, Ammonites, Edomites, Zidonians, and Hittites; of the nations concerning which the Lord said unto the children of Israel, Ye shall not go in to them, neither shall they come in unto you: for surely they will turn away your heart after their gods: Solomon clave unto these in love. And he had seven hundred wives, princesses, and three hundred concubines: and his wives turned away his heart. For it came to pass, when Solomon was old, that his wives turned away his heart after other gods: and his heart was not perfect with the Lord his God, as was the heart of David his father (1 Kings 11:1-4).

Like Solomon, many of us love to court the forbidden. We think we can do so and continue to be the voice of godly influence only to discover we were standing upon a slippery bank of destruction. The relationships you have will determine what is being deposited in your spirit.

  ⡝ *Whoever has access to your mind will have great influence over your life, for better or for worse.* Whoever you hang around with will get inside your head. Sometimes you will be aware of this, but more often it will be subliminal, entering you and affecting your mind without your conscious awareness. Often these influences are invisible and unspoken. They can be mannerisms, character strengths or flaws, and mode of operation—all subliminally being passed down to you.

  ⡝ *Who you associate with is a prediction of your future.* "Do not be fooled: 'Bad friends will ruin good habits'" (1 Cor. 15:33 NCV). The Weymouth New Testament says it this way, "Do not deceive yourselves: Evil companionships corrupt good morals."

We see in the life of David that some of his men were known as *sons of Belial.* This term means worthless. That tells us there are worthless associations and there are worthy associations. "He that walketh with wise men shall be wise: but a companion of fools shall be destroyed" (Prov. 13:20).

  ⡝ *The wisdom of God or the wiles of satan are imparted through those you associate with.* Who you choose to associate with will determine what flows to and through you.

People are containers. They are either vessels of glory or vessels of grief. Jesus poured His words and wisdom into His disciples. Through his epistles, Paul poured the wisdom of God into the lives of Timothy and Titus as well as, our lives. Elisha followed Elijah, and Joshua followed Moses. The wisdom in Moses was imparted to Joshua and Elijah's anointing flowed through to Elisha.

Promotion or destruction come through those you choose to associate with. Your association will be the basis of the pleasure or pain in your life. Who is your closest association? What does that person bring into your life? What impact will that person have on your life? Is that person stirring your faith? Is that person causing you to grasp the greatness of God?

Who you associate with
will be the basis of the pleasure
or pain in your life.

Who Should You Associate With?

First and foremost, you should associate with God through His Word—the Bible—and prayer. Your utmost and obvious priority in life should be to learn to protect and cultivate your relationship with God. Don't try to figure Him out with your senses or emotions. Many years ago Smith Wigglesworth stated, "I do not understand God by my feelings and emotions but I understand God by His words." Job 22:21 says, "Acquaint now thyself with him, and be at peace: thereby good shall come unto thee."

Your second association should be with godly men and women who possess what you do not but would love to have. Find a godly mentor. Find people smarter or more anointed than you are, hang around them, and discover what they know.

Of course we are to love everyone, but we are not to invest our time with everyone. Beyond your immediate family, you have to choose who you will let into your life and who will keep out. I made up my mind long ago that I will live at peace with all men but not all men will have access to my life, mind, and heart. If you allow some people into your life, they will be nothing but a weight or barnacle that you have to carry, and they will slow you down. "Wherefore seeing we also are compassed about with so great a cloud of witnesses, let us lay aside every weight, and the sin which doth so easily beset us, and let us run with patience the race that is set before us" (Heb. 12:1).

There are people who will be an unnecessary weight in your life. As soon as you enter into a wrong relationship, you will quickly realize this. Life is already complicated. You have to face satan and his cohorts, and now you have the weight of this relationship to deal with as well. You may feel like you have to help that person, but you will soon understand that you can't help everyone and not everyone wants your help.

What I realized, and this became a revelation to me, is this. I am a Christian but I am not the Messiah. Jesus is the Messiah. From now on you have to weigh and evaluate the authenticity of every person who has access to your life. Paul masterfully wrote, "Be not deceived: evil communications corrupt good manners" (1 Cor. 15:33). There are three interesting words in this verse. They are *deceived, evil,* and *corrupt.*

The word *deceived* in Greek is *planao,* and it means:

- To be led aside from the path of virtue, to go astray, sin
- To sever or fall away from the truth
- Make that which is wrong look right
- Fail to admit to oneself that something is true

> What I realized, and this became a revelation to me, is this. I am a Christian but I am not the Messiah. Jesus is the Messiah.

There are people in our lives that are wrong but made to look right, and we have failed to admit to ourselves that these people are only there to drain us and take advantage of us. Even as you read this book, ask yourself if there is someone in your life who is taking you away from your God-given call. Are you willing to admit that?

The word *evil* is the Greek word *kakos*, and it means:

- That which is inherently evil
- Of a bad nature
- Troublesome
- Injurious, pernicious, destructive, baneful

This word refers to *that which is evil and desires to spread evil.* When you come in contact with it, it brings defilement to one's life. You need to realize that there are people around you who are bent on doing evil, for that is what they are. They may have been your best friend in the past, but they are not now. Your best friend would not take you down the road of sin. Your best friend is the one who brings the best out of you. If you know someone who continues to practice evil, you need to walk away. Do not think to yourself, "I'm a strong believer and I can handle it." The simple truth for you to consider is this, "You are not and neither should you try to be wiser than God." Listen to the wisdom of Solomon, "Can a man take fire in his bosom, and his clothes not be burned?" (Prov. 6:27). If you play with fire you will get burned.

The third word, *corrupt*, means that which destroys gradually and becomes debase. Pay attention to this. The wrong relationship is slowly changing your thoughts and dulling your sensitivity to sin— without you even realizing it. When you do realize it, it could be too late. Do not get into that kind of situation. Value your life and value desire to increase in anointing by choosing godly relationships.

Chapter 10

IMPARTATION

Impartation is very significant in our quest to increase in the anointing. Romans 1:11 says, "For I long to see you, that I may impart unto you some spiritual gift, to the end ye may be established." The Weymouth New Testament says it this way, "For I am longing to see you, in order to convey to you some spiritual help, so that you may be strengthened."

We hear a lot about impartation these days, but unfortunately most believers do not have a clue what this really entails. Some think that if they go to one service and a man lays hands on them, they have received an impartation of anointing. Now I am not demeaning this practice, but impartation is more than a man laying hands on you one time and all of a sudden you are Superman. *That may be the exception, but it is not necessarily the rule.*

In our days of modern technology where speed is everything, we think we can find a speedy way to get to the anointing. But impartation is not an instant downloading of another's man's gift. If that man had to pay the price of time and devotion before God to obtain his anointing, what makes you think you won't be required to do the same? There is a price to pay. There is a major difference between transference and impartation. Transference is instant but impartation requires time. Impartation is gradual and birthed out of relationship. We see this in the lives of Elijah and Elisha:

> *The Lord said unto him, Go, return on thy way to the wilderness of Damascus: and when thou comest, anoint Hazael to be king over Syria: And Jehu the son of Nimshi shalt thou anoint to be king over Israel: and Elisha the son of Shaphat of Abelmeholah shalt thou anoint to be prophet in thy room. And it shall come to pass, that him that escapeth the sword of Hazael shall Jehu slay: and him that escapeth from the sword of Jehu shall Elisha slay. Yet I have left me seven thousand in Israel, all the knees which have not bowed unto Baal, and every mouth which hath not kissed him. So he departed thence, and found Elisha the son of Shaphat, who was plowing with twelve yoke of oxen before him, and he with the twelfth: and Elijah passed by him, and cast his mantle upon him. And he left the oxen, and ran after Elijah, and said, Let me, I pray thee, kiss my father and my mother, and then I will follow thee. And he said unto him, Go back again: for what have I done to thee? And he returned back from him, and took a yoke of oxen, and slew them, and boiled their flesh with the instruments of the oxen, and gave unto the people, and they did eat. Then he arose, and went after Elijah, and ministered unto him* (1 Kings 19 15-21).

I want you to notice the words, *"Elijah passed by him* [Elisha] *and cast his mantle on him."* The mantle had a dual meaning—the anointing and the office. God specifically tells us in His Word that He does not anoint flesh. God anoints the mantle that is representative of the office in which a person is to operate.

> *[Use this oil also to] Anoint Aaron and his sons and consecrate them so they may serve Me as priests. Say to the Israelites, This is to be My sacred anointing oil for the generations to come. Do not pour it on anyone else's body and do not make any other oil using the same formula. It is sacred, and you are to consider it sacred* (Exodus 30:30-32 TNIV).

Then dress Aaron in the sacred garments, anoint him and consecrate him so he may serve Me as priest. Bring his sons and dress them in tunics. Anoint them just as you anointed their father, so they may serve Me as priests. Their anointing will be to a priesthood that will continue throughout their generations (Exodus 40:13-15 TNIV).

The impartation took place by the transfer of a garment. God puts the garment on the man and passes it down to the one who serves Him. We understand that Elisha followed Elijah and ministered to him for twenty years. That means Elijah was the mentor and Elisha was the protégé. This is very important in your desire to increase in the anointing.

We live in a time when no one wants to submit to anyone. Everyone wants to be the "commander-in-chief." Especially in our Spirit-filled circle, there is the sense that we don't have to answer to anyone. Our excuse is that "I am led by the Spirit." As great and truthful a statement as this is, most people use it to excuse their rebellion and lack of accountability. We also use expressions like, "God spoke to me," or "The Lord told me this," when it clearly was not the Lord.

The voice of God will never violate the principles of God. The Bible is the infallible Word of God containing principles God expects us to live by. His principles are to be the first and final authority in our lives. There are principles for health, wealth, business, church, and ministry. One of the most important principles we see in the Bible is the principle of *impartation through mentoring*. We see this again and again in the Scriptures. Here are a few examples.

The voice of God will never violate the principles of God.

🌿 *Moses and Joshua—the impartation of wisdom and leadership.* "And Joshua the son of Nun was full of the spirit of wisdom; for Moses had laid his hands upon him: and the children of Israel hearkened unto him, and did as the Lord commanded Moses" (Deut. 34:9).

❧ *Naomi and Ruth—the impartation of a wealthy place.* "And Naomi had a kinsman of her husband's, a mighty man of wealth, of the family of Elimelech; and his name was Boaz" (Ruth 2:1).

❧ *Elijah and Elisha—the impartation of a double portion.*

Elisha saw it, and he cried, My father, my father, the chariot of Israel, and the horsemen thereof. And he saw him no more: and he took hold of his own clothes, and rent them in two pieces. He took up also the mantle of Elijah that fell from him, and went back, and stood by the bank of Jordan; and he took the mantle of Elijah that fell from him, and smote the waters, and said, Where is the Lord God of Elijah? and when he also had smitten the waters, they parted hither and thither: and Elisha went over. And when the sons of the prophets which were to view at Jericho saw him, they said, The spirit of Elijah doth rest on Elisha (2 Kings 2:12-15).

❧ *David and his men—the impartation of strength and might to men who once were weak.*

David therefore departed thence, and escaped to the cave Adullam: and when his brethren and all his father's house heard it, they went down thither to him. And every one that was in distress, and every one that was in debt, and every one that was discontented, gathered themselves unto him; and he became a captain over them: and there were with him about four hundred men (1 Samuel 22:1-2).

Now let's look at Second Samuel 23:8, which says, "These be the names *of the mighty men whom David had.*"

❧ *Jesus and the disciples—the impartation turned weak and worldly men into the foundational apostles of the Lamb.* "Now when they saw the boldness of Peter and John, and perceived that they were unlearned and ignorant men, they marveled; and they took knowledge of them, that they had been with Jesus" (Acts 4:13).

○∞ *Barnabas and Paul—the impartation turned a wicked man into a Word man.*

But Barnabas took him, and brought him to the apostles, and declared unto them how he had seen the Lord in the way, and that He had spoken to him, and how he had preached boldly at Damascus in the name of Jesus. And he was with them coming in and going out at Jerusalem. And he spake boldly in the name of the Lord Jesus (Acts 9:27-29).

○∞ *Paul and Timothy—the impartation from a spiritual father to his spiritual son.* "Paul, an apostle of Jesus Christ by the commandment of God our Savior, and Lord Jesus Christ, which is our hope; unto Timothy, my own son in the faith" (1 Tim. 1:1-2).

Paul's instructions:

- "The things that thou hast heard of me among many witnesses, *the same commit thou to faithful men,* who shall be able to teach others also" (2 Tim. 2:2).

- In The Message, we read, "Pass on what you heard from me—the whole congregation saying Amen!— to reliable leaders who are competent to teach others."

- The New Living Translation says, "You have heard me teach things that have been confirmed by many reliable witnesses. Now teach these great truths to other trustworthy people who will be able to pass them on to others."

- The New International Version says in Philippians 4:9, "Whatever you have learned or received or heard from me, or seen in me—put it into practice. And the God of peace will be with you."

- The King James Version says, "Those things, which ye have both learned, and received, and heard, and seen in me, do: and the God of peace shall be with you."

"The things which I have taught you, pass it to other men." The principle of mentoring is not a new business concept, but one of the

oldest and best methods of learning. In Bible times, this was the primary way wisdom, skill, and spirituality were passed from one generation to the next. *Mentoring* is simply the imparting and transmitting of knowledge, wisdom, and skill development to an apprentice or protégé. This would fulfill Solomon's writing, "iron sharpeneth iron." I love the Good News rendition of Proverbs 27:17, which says, "People learn from one another, just as iron sharpens iron."

A mentor is a pioneer who has already ventured into an area and is now able to pass on his knowledge, expertise, and experience to a protégée. Usually the protégé is younger and the mentor is an older individual who imparts his wisdom to the novice. Simply put, mentoring is the primary medium or bedrock for leadership development.

The impartation of wisdom and the wisdom of impartation through mentoring was also used to prevent the possible damage that could be caused by the zeal and inexperience of the novice. A great mistake that many churches make these days is their tendency to entrust a position of authority to a novice. The Bible clearly forbids it! It does not matter that the person has a tremendous testimony and that his testimony could bless an untold number of people. That is not the criteria for position.

> The impartation of wisdom and the wisdom of impartation through mentoring was also used to prevent the possible damage that could be caused by the zeal and inexperience of the novice.

The Term "Mentor"

Mentoring is not a new concept. It has been around for generations. In fact you have been mentored all your life whether you realize it or not. There are three major kinds of mentoring:

- *Parental mentoring.* Your very first mentors were your parents.

- *Professional mentoring.* You received this kind through your school teachers, lecturers, and employers.

- *Pastoral or prophetic mentoring.* This is information and formation that comes through your pastor or anointed servant of God.

The first recorded use of the term "mentor" can be traced to a French book entitled *Les Aventures de Telemaque*, by French author François Fénelon. In the book, the lead character is that of Mentor, a close friend of Odysseus, who goes to war at the time of the birth of his son Telemachus. The Mentor trains Telemachus to grow into adulthood and eventually assume his royal responsibilities.

Les Aventures de Telemaque was published in 1699. It was very popular during the eighteenth century. The modern application of the term "mentor," as per this publication means: a trusted friend, counselor, or teacher, usually a more experienced person. The quality of your mentor will determine the success that flows in your life. The impartation your mentor gives to you will determine how high you go in life. That's why you have to be very wise about who you choose to mentor you. Your associations will determine your assimilation and impartation. You need to realize that you need a mentor.

Your associations will determine your assimilation and impartation.

The Ministry of Impartation

God, in order to equip us for maximum impact on our generation, has given us the "ministry of impartation," which is the ability to give unto others that which God has given to us. The two main intentions of mentoring and impartation are service and spiritual gifts.

Through the ministry of mentoring and impartation, we receive the extra edge that will help us function in a much greater way in the supernatural. We are able to learn from the experience and mistakes of someone who has already walked where we are preparing to walk. We could learn things the hard way, but why would we do that when the Lord has made it possible for us to be empowered spiritually by impartation from those who already carry a recognized ministry and the anointing in the Holy Spirit.

God, in His endeavor to shape us into the image of Christ, will use the union of divine purpose and human vessel. He uses mentors to stretch us, encourage us, and hold us accountable or responsible. In the process, our giftings are unlocked. Basically, a mentor's job is to teach you the ropes.

The word *mentor* is used a lot these days, especially in Spirit-filled circles, but so far we have not seen the reality of it. Many use it as a title of grandeur, but the application is missing. The purpose of mentoring and impartation is to strengthen or establish or, in more basic terms, the art of discipleship. "For I long to see you, that I may impart unto you some spiritual gift, to the end ye may be established" (Rom. 1:11).

The apostle Paul was eager to impart spiritual gifts to the Roman believers. I want you to notice the word *gift*. The Greek word is *charisma* and according to *Strong's Concordance*, it means "grace or gifts denoting extraordinary powers, distinguishing certain Christians and enabling them to serve the church of Christ, the reception of which is due to the power of divine grace operating on their souls by the Holy Spirit."

> The purpose of mentoring and impartation is to strengthen or establish.

The apostle Paul wanted to impart or release from the Holy Spirit a supernatural gift that would motivate certain believers to more effectively serve the Body of Christ and give them a supernatural edge. We see Paul reminding Timothy of this impartation in his life.

"Wherefore I put thee in remembrance that thou stir up the gift of God, *which is in thee by the putting on of my hands"* (2 Tim. 1:6).

Again we see the word *gift* used in connection with impartation and laying on of hands. Paul deposited a gift in the life of Timothy through laying on of hands. Moses did the same thing with Joshua: "And Joshua the son of Nun *was full of the spirit of wisdom; for Moses had laid his hands upon him:* and the children of Israel hearkened unto him, and did as the Lord commanded Moses" (Deut. 34:9). *"And Moses did as the Lord commanded him: and he took Joshua, and set him before Eleazar the priest, and before all the congregation: And he laid his hands upon him,* and gave him a charge, as the Lord commanded by the hand of Moses" (Num. 27:22-23).

The spirit of wisdom was imparted in the life of Joshua through the laying of Moses' hands. In studying the word, you will find several ways that impartation takes place.

> ✎ *The first step to receiving an impartation from your mentor is developing and maintaining a close relationship.* Elisha followed Elijah for twenty years. He stayed with his spiritual father and served him closely while the sons of the prophets were far off. They knew when Elijah's time was coming, but they never received the blessing of a double portion.
>
> Joshua had a close relationship with Moses and he was called Moses' minister (See Joshua 1:1.) Matthew Henry's *Commentary* states:
>
> "He was Moses' minister, that is, an immediate attendant upon his person and assistant in business. The Septuagint translates it "hypourgos," a workman under Moses, under his direction and command. Observe, 1. He that was here called to honor had been long bred to business... 2. He was trained up in subjection and under command. Those are fittest to rule that have learned to obey. 3. He that was to succeed Moses was intimately acquainted with him, that he might fully know his doctrine and manner of life, his purpose and

long-suffering (2 Timothy 3:10), might take the same measures, walk in the same spirit, in the same steps, having to carry on the same work."

The word *minister* also denotes the idea of actual and personal attendance upon a superior.

℞ *The second step to receiving an impartation from your mentor is the laying on of hands.* We see that both Moses, Paul, Peter, and John laid hands on believers and imparted gifts to them.

Deuteronomy 34:9 says, "And Joshua the son of Nun *was full of the spirit of wisdom; for Moses had laid his hands upon him:* and the children of Israel hearkened unto him, and did as the Lord commanded Moses." While Second Timothy 1:6 tells us, "Wherefore I put thee in remembrance that thou stir up the gift of God, which *is in thee by the putting on of my hands.*" Finally, in Acts 8:14-18, we read:

When the apostles which were at Jerusalem heard that Samaria had received the word of God, they sent unto them Peter and John: Who, when they were come down, prayed for them, that they might receive the Holy Ghost: (For as yet He was fallen upon none of them: only they were baptized in the name of the Lord Jesus.) Then laid they their hands on them, and they received the Holy Ghost. And when Simon saw that through laying on of the apostles' hands the Holy Ghost was given, he offered them money.

A Word of Caution

The laying on of hands is activated through contact and transmission. Once contact is made, something is transmitted or transferred. Do not let everybody and anybody lay hands on you as you do not know what spirit they are carrying or what sin is in their lives which may be transferred to you. Many desperate people are running here and there looking for someone to lay hands on them, but this is a dangerous practice as they might easily get more than they bargained for. Be cautious about who you allow to lay hands on you.

Prophecy or Prophetic Utterance

Let's look at a few scriptures. "Neglect not the gift that is in thee, which was given thee by prophecy, with the laying on of the hands of the presbytery" (1 Tim. 4:14). "This charge I commit unto thee, son Timothy, according to the prophecies which went before on thee, that thou by them mightest war a good warfare" (1 Tim. 1:18). Finally from 1 Samuel 10:5-6:

> *After that thou shalt come to the hill of God, where is the garrison of the Philistines: and it shall come to pass, when thou art come thither to the city, that thou shalt meet a company of prophets coming down from the high place with a psaltery, and a tabret, and a pipe, and a harp, before them; and they shall prophesy: And the Spirit of the Lord will come upon thee, and thou shalt prophesy with them, and shalt be turned into another man.*

Assimilation of Instructions

It is obvious if you read the materials and listen to a certain Bible teacher or group, you will assimilate and believe what is being taught. The information received becomes your impartation.

How does this apply to you?

Find a man or woman of God from whom you can receive mentoring. This person does not need to be your best friend, but it should be a person of prayer with a strong anointing—your pastor or some other person of the Word. Find a mentor who is where you would like to be, because his present will be your future. Let us look at the lives of Elijah and Elisha. Elijah was the mentor and Elisha was the protégé. He followed Elijah, stayed with him, and served him for twenty years. He had a close relationship with the prophet of God. Impartation is birthed out of relationship, and Elisha wanted a double portion of what Elijah had. This does not necessarily mean that Elisha wanted to outdo Elijah in a competitive manner. The term *double portion* was used to refer to the blessings given to the firstborn son from the father. Elisha received the blessing of a son. We already know that Elisha had a natural father and mother and yet he called Elijah his father. Consider these scriptures:

> *He departed thence, and found Elisha the son of Shaphat, who was plowing with twelve yoke of oxen before him, and he with the twelfth: and Elijah passed by him, and cast his mantle upon him. And he left the oxen, and ran after Elijah, and said, Let me, I pray thee, kiss my father and my mother, and then I will follow thee* (1 Kings 19:19-20).

> *It came to pass, as they still went on, and talked, that, behold, there appeared a chariot of fire, and horses of fire, and parted them both asunder; and Elijah went up by a whirlwind into heaven. And Elisha saw it, and he cried, My father, my father, the chariot of Israel, and the horsemen thereof* (2 Kings 2:11-12).

> *Elisha saw it, and he cried, My father, my father, the chariot of Israel, and the horsemen thereof. And he saw him no more: and he took hold of his own clothes, and rent them in two pieces. He took up also the mantle of Elijah that fell from him, and went back, and stood by the bank of Jordan; and he took the mantle of Elijah that fell from him, and smote the waters, and said, Where is the Lord God of Elijah? and when he also had smitten the waters, they parted hither and thither: and Elisha went over. And when the sons of the prophets which were to view at Jericho saw him, they said, The spirit of Elijah doth rest on Elisha* (2 Kings 2:12-15).

The double portion belonged to Elisha because he followed and ministered to Elijah closely as a son would, whereas the sons of the prophets followed from a distance and only showed up when Elijah was about to pass on the mantle. Impartation comes as a result of close relationship. The sons of the prophets could only testify that Elisha received the impartation.

Life Application

Get involved in your local church and develop a great relationship with your pastor. If that does not meet your needs, then look at alternatives. Growing up as a teenager, I knew what I wanted to achieve in life and what I was called to do. I had to look for mentors to impart into my life. Mentoring and impartation can be personal or distant. By distant, I mean through resources such as books, audio teachings, and conferences. I read Kenneth Hagin's books voraciously as a teenager and listened to hundreds of Kenneth Copeland's teachings—still do. These two men, especially Kenneth Copeland, had a great impact on my life. Although I am not personally acquainted with them, I am forever grateful for what they imparted in my life. To this day, even though I listen and learn from many others, I still have a special fondness for these two great men of God. "For though ye have ten thousand instructors in Christ, yet have ye not many fathers: for in Christ Jesus I have begotten you through the gospel" (1 Cor. 4:15). *How to choose a mentor?* Your mentor is where you would like to be in the future. As important as success is, the most important criteria are character and a fatherly attitude.

Allow me to list a few things to look for when choosing a mentor.

⚞ *A mentor should be fatherly.* "For though ye have ten thousand instructors in Christ, yet have ye not many fathers: for in Christ Jesus I have begotten you through the gospel" (1 Cor. 4:15). The number one thing I look for in a mentor is his quality as a father figure. I may listen to many instructors but I can only have one father. Again, this is a term used so commonly in Spirit-filled circles. Many claim to be "spiritual fathers," but the only thing they do is receive financially from their spiritual sons. The sowing is only going toward the father and not toward the sons. Mentoring is not just a business trade; it is also a spiritual transaction. While I don't have a problem with spiritual sons blessing their fathers in the faith, it is imperative those fathers also bless their sons. That is the responsibility of a father. "A good man leaveth an inheritance to his children's children" (Prov. 13:22).

Paul said that he had begotten the Corinthians. Living in our modern world, we see many fragmented homes and children with absent fathers. The truth is that just having a child does not make you a father. A father is not only one who seeded into a womb but one who stayed around and nurtured his child until he or she became a mature adult. A *spiritual* father is not only one who seeds the Word of God into your spirit but one who also takes the time to nurture, build, and correct you. "Furthermore we have had fathers of our flesh which corrected us, and we gave them reverence" (Heb. 12:9).

We see the relationship of father and son in the lives and ministries of Elijah and Elisha. Elisha served Elijah in the ministry and received the blessing reserved for a son by his father—the double portion.

We see the same pattern in the life of Moses and Joshua. *"And Joshua the son of Nun was full of the spirit of wisdom; for Moses had laid his hands upon him: and the children of Israel hearkened unto him, and did as the Lord commanded Moses"* (Deut. 34:9).

A mentor should be a positive role model.

For yourselves know how ye ought to follow us: for we behaved not ourselves disorderly among you; neither did we eat any man's bread for nought; but wrought with labour and travail night and day, that we might not be chargeable to any of you: Not because we have not power, but to make ourselves an ensample unto you to follow us (2 Thessalonians 3:7-9).

A mentor should be a man or woman of godly character. In their quest to be mentored, many choose people with great charisma rather than great character. While they may be blessed by the charisma, the flawed character will be imparted as well. There are no perfect ministers, of course, none but Christ. However you must take a long look at who and what you are following. Is there anger? Is there a problem with the opposite sex? Is there financial integrity? Is the mentor a person of his word? This is so important yet overlooked by many believers. Let's look at Proverbs 22:24-25 in three versions to get a clearer picture of what God has to say about this.

- The King James Version says, "Make no friendship with an angry man; and with a furious man thou shalt not go: Lest thou learn his ways, and get a snare to thy soul."

- The New Living Testament says, "Don't befriend angry people or associate with hot-tempered people, or you will learn to be like them and endanger your soul."

- The Good News Bible says, "Don't make friends with people who have hot, violent tempers. You might learn their habits and not be able to change."

❧ *A mentor should have longevity and fruit in his or her ministry.* How long has your possible mentor been around? Can you see the fruit of their labor? We are not to follow a novice. The old saying, "Time tells the truth" is also true when it comes to ministry. Longevity motivates trust. Fruit or results reveal expertise in their field.

❧ *A mentor should provide insights, instruction, and revelation.* Your mentor should be able to give you access to information that will take you to the next level in your life and ministry.

Hear, ye children, the instruction of a father, and attend to know understanding. For I give you good doctrine, forsake ye not my law. For I was my father's son, tender and only beloved in the sight of my mother. He taught me also, and said unto me, Let thine heart retain my words: keep my commandments, and live. Get wisdom, get understanding:

forget it not; neither decline from the words of my mouth (Proverbs 4:1-5).

Your mentor's purpose is to establish a relationship with you (if possible) to release and watch over your potential and purpose. However if a relationship is not possible due to distance and other reasons, but you are gleaning from their teachings, then it is important that you are receiving information and insights to release your potential.

☞ *A mentor should challenge and uproot mediocrity from your life.* A mentor is someone who with God's help and grace turns your potential into actual power and helps you realize your dream. That doesn't mean, however, that your mentor should pat you on your back for your mediocrity. A friend might put up with your lack of excellence, but that isn't the role of a mentor. His purpose is to make sure you produce fruit acceptable to your calling.

I do not expect my mentor to justify my flaws and condone my mediocrity. I expect him to challenge my lack of fruit and excellence. I expect my mentor to work me and drill into me the spirit of excellence and help me get results.

Many Christians want to be mentored without being challenged. But this is impossible. If you want to go to the next level, you must learn to accept correction. I may not like everything they do or say but I respect their authority in my life.

I have had many mentors in my life but the ones that made a positive and profound impact on my life were Kenneth Copeland, Kenneth E. Hagin, Frederick K.C. Price, Chris Tunde Joda, and Bishop David Oyedepo. From Kenneth Copeland and Kenneth Hagin, I learned the Word. But I learned ministry and how to impact a service from Dr. Joda. He was a phenomenal teacher and worker who stretched me in Africa. In fact he was the door that God used for me to enter Nigeria and the USA. I will always thank God for his life and the good he worked in my life.

I remember being with him on a ten-day trip. In that time, I ministered thirty-nine times. After ten days, I was ready to go home, and yet he had the audacity to ask me if I wanted to stay longer. I faintly replied, "No! I have nothing else to say to you people. Fold me and put me in my suitcase and send me back home." He had me preaching four services daily. And he would always say, "Are you ready to make trouble for the devil?" He stretched me. I did not back down when he gave me the schedule. I never complained. I knew what it was doing for me. He gave me books to read, and when I was not ministering my day was spent listening to teachings and watching preaching videos! I saw a man addicted to ministry and the Word!

I will forever be grateful for my mentors. Some I know personally and some I don't, but they are all precious to me.

Chapter 11

ADORATION

Every believer or minister who desires to increase in the anointing must live a life of worship. Adoration is worship unto God our Creator. Worship is not just something we do; it is the very purpose of our existence. We were created to bring pleasure to God, and worship brings pleasure to Him. In short, we have been made to minister unto the Lord. It is about being a priest before the Lord. Ministering unto the Lord was the priority ministry of the priest in the Old Testament, and that should be our first ministry as a royal priesthood. Let's look at some scriptures concerning this principle:

- "Thou art worthy, O Lord, to receive glory and honour and power: for *Thou hast created all things, and for Thy pleasure they are and were created*" (Rev. 4:11).

- "The Lord hath made all things for Himself" (Prov. 16:4).

- "This people have I formed for Myself; they shall shew forth My praise" (Isa. 43:21).

- "For of Him, and through Him, and to Him, are all things: to whom be glory for ever. Amen" (Rom. 11:36).

"...now is, when the true worshippers shall worship the Father in spirit and in truth: for the Father seeketh such to worship Him" (John 4:23).

> We were created to bring pleasure to God, and worship brings pleasure to Him.

Bringing pleasure to God is called worship. The Bible says, *"The Lord is pleased only with those who worship Him and trust His love"* (Ps. 147:11 CEV). Our ultimate goal in life is to please God. A life of worship is a life that is grateful to God.

However, many times in our lives, pride sets in and we stop worshiping God as we used to. In the King James Version there is a term that is used over and over in the book of Psalms and Proverbs. It is, "the fear of the Lord." We understand this phrase to mean "reverence." Literally thought, in Hebrew "the fear of the Lord" can be better translated as "the worship of the Lord." So when the psalmist says, "The fear of the Lord is the beginning of wisdom" (Ps. 111:10), we can translate that as "The worship of the Lord is the beginning of wisdom."

Your first act of wisdom is to worship God and give Him the praise and glory that is due His name. Praise brings the presence of God, but worship secures the longevity of His presence. I don't know about you, but I love to be in the presence of God. I crave the presence of God in my life. I want His touch on everything I do. There are three things that I constantly crave and pursue in life:

1. The Word of God
2. Praying in the Holy Ghost
3. Reality of his presence through praise and worship

> Your first act of wisdom is to worship God and give him the praise and glory that is due His name.

The Father is looking for true worshipers—those who will worship Him unashamedly. Worship will usher in an atmosphere of miracles and the supernatural. There is an interesting story in the Gospel of Mark that I want to bring to your attention.

> *When Jesus was passed over again by ship unto the other side, much people gathered unto Him: and He was nigh unto the sea. And, behold, there cometh one of the rulers of the synagogue, Jairus by name; and when he saw Him, he fell at his feet, and besought Him greatly, saying, My little daughter lieth at the point of death: I pray Thee, come and lay thy hands on her, that she may be healed; and she shall live. And Jesus went with Him; and much people followed him, and thronged Him* (Mark 5:21-24).

The Worship of Jairus and the Wonder That Followed

Much good has been taught about the faith of Jairus, and rightly so. However, I want you to notice something else remarkable about this ruler of the synagogue. First of all, note that the name *Jairus* means "He who God enlightens." The psalmist tells us, "The entrance of Thy words giveth light" (Psalm 119:130). So we know that Jairus had some light operating in him even though he was in a dark situation with his deathly sick daughter.

Now notice what Jairus did when he came to Jesus. "*When he saw Him, he fell at His feet.*" That is the posture of worship, adoration, and dependency. In Eastern culture, to fall at someone's feet suggests, "*I respect you, I know you are higher than me, and I need your blessing.*"

> In Eastern culture,
> to fall at the feet of somebody is suggesting,
> "I respect you, I know you are higher
> than me, and I need your blessing."

Understand that Jairus held a good position in the community as a ruler of the synagogue. He could have allowed pride to stop him from coming to Jesus and bowing at His feet. But he didn't. When Jairus threw himself at the feet of Jesus, his actions were saying, *"Lord, I humble myself before you, I need you, and I depend on you, for you are my only hope."*

After falling at Jesus' feet, notice what Jairus requested of Him, "I pray Thee, *come and lay Thy hands on her,* that she may be healed; and she shall live." Jairus made a demand upon the hand of Jesus. When the Scriptures talks about the hand of God, it is always a manifestation of His supernatural power. Before Jairus made a demand upon the hand of Jesus, he fell at His feet. The way to activate the hand of Jesus is to fall at His feet. This means to humble yourself, be dependent on, and be a worshiper of God. When Jairus did so, we read that Jesus followed him home and raised his daughter from the dead.

When worship becomes the order of the day in your life, God will follow you. He follows the worshiper. He will come to your house, and everything that is dead in your house will be made alive. Remember these statements about worship:

- ❦ *Worship* brings life to a dead situation.
- ❦ *Worship* will excite God to follow you to your house. He will leave the multitude to follow the one worshiper.
- ❦ *Worship* secures the hand of God in your life.
- ❦ *Worship* will restore that which was lost.
- ❦ *Worship* will remove reproach and mockery from your house.

From Jesus Christ, who is the faithful witness, and the first begotten of the dead, and the Prince of the kings of the earth. Unto Him that loved us, and washed us from our sins in His own blood, and hath made us kings and priests unto God and His Father; to Him be glory and dominion for ever and ever. Amen (Revelation 1:5-6).

Ministering Unto the Lord

As a priest, the believer's first ministry is unto the Lord in worship and adoration. This is where we renew our strength like an eagle as we wait upon Him. "They that *wait upon the Lord* shall renew their strength; they shall mount up with wings as eagles; they shall run and not be weary; and they shall walk and not faint" (Isa. 40:31).

To wait upon the Lord means to stay in His presence in a state of simple adoration. To *wait* is defined in the dictionary as:

- To stay in one place or do nothing for a period of time until something happens or in the expectation that something will happen
- To remain or rest in expectation
- To remain and be in readiness

The believer's ministry is threefold:

- *Ministering* unto the Lord
- *Ministering* from the Word
- *Ministering* to the people

Today in our quest for church growth, many have focused on "ministering to the people" at the expense of "ministering unto the Lord." Effective ministering to people cannot be achieved without first ministering to the Lord. The early apostles knew this reality when faced with the challenges of church growth. In Acts 6:1-2,4 we read:

> *In those days, when the number of the disciples was multiplied, there arose a murmuring of the Grecians against the Hebrews, because their widows were **neglected in the daily ministration**. Then the twelve called the multitude of the disciples unto them, and said, **It is not reason that we should leave the word of God, and serve tables** ... But we will give ourselves continually to prayer, and to the ministry of the word.*

You see the apostles held "ministering unto the Lord" above "ministering to the people." That is not to say that "ministering to the people" is unimportant. It's just that you cannot touch people if you have not first been touched by God. We see this in the earthly ministry of Jesus. He never allowed the crowd to dictate His steps when it came to spending time in the presence of His Father. "But so much the more went there *a fame abroad of Him: and great multitudes came together to hear,* and to be healed by Him of their infirmities. And *He withdrew Himself into the wilderness, and prayed"* (Luke 5:15-16).

You cannot touch people if you
have not first been touched by God.

Great multitudes came to see Jesus as His fame spread throughout the land. But notice what He did. He was more committed to be in the presence of His Father than the people. Of course when we read the Gospels, we see that Jesus spent time with many people but He made sure that He spent more time with His Father. Ministering unto the Lord came first as these Scriptures show:

- Immediately after the feeding of the 5000

  Straightway Jesus constrained His disciples to get into a ship, and to go before Him unto the other side, while He sent the multitudes away. And when He had sent the multitudes away, He went up into a mountain apart to pray: and when the evening was come, He was there alone (Matthew 14:22-23).

- After a great healing crusade

  "And in the morning, rising up a great while before day, He went out, and departed into a solitary place, and there prayed" (Mark 1:35).

- Before He made important decisions

  "And it came to pass in those days, that He went out into a mountain to pray, and continued all night in prayer to God" (Luke 6:12).

Your effectiveness
in life and ministry is connected
to your fellowship with God.

Be a worshiper of God and let His presence come into your house as when the ark of God was left in the house of Obededom the Gittite. The ark, which typified the presence of God, remained in his house for three months, bringing blessing to him and to all his household.

The ark of the Lord continued in the house of Obededom the Gittite three months: and the Lord blessed Obededom, and all his household. And it was told king David, saying, The Lord hath blessed the house of Obededom, and all that pertaineth unto him, because of the ark of God. So David went and brought up the ark of God from the house of Obededom into the city of David with gladness (2 Samuel 6:11-12).

Through your adoration of God, His presence will invade your life, home, and everything that belongs to you. The result will be blessings all over.

Chapter 12

DEDICATION

In 2008, the world watched in amazement and wonder as Michael Phelps earned an incredible eight gold medals in the Beijing Olympics. What a remarkable feat! Long after he is gone from this world, people will remember. Even if he never repeats this accomplishment or attends another Olympic Games, his name will be in the record books and he will be remembered as a great swimmer.

So what made what Michael Phelps did so spectacular? Eight gold medals did not just drop in his lap; he had to be dedicated to his daily, strict regimen of training for five hours a day, six days a week. As a nine-year-old, Phelps was diagnosed with ADHD (Attention Deficit Hyperactivity Disorder), and yet he did not allow this setback to stop him from becoming a great Olympian. There must have been times when he wanted to do something other than swimming, but dedication to his dream kept him in the pool.

Zig Ziglar aptly said, "The tougher you are on yourself, the easier life will be on you. The easier you are on yourself, the tougher life will be on you." When Phelps was interviewed by NBC, he revealed, "Eat, sleep, swim, that's all I do." His total dedication brought him to

157

a place of distinction. When you are dedicated, you will also have a place of distinction in life.

Whether your field is ministry or business, it makes no difference to God. Increase and distinction come through dedication. If you want an increase in the anointing, then your level of dedication to God, your call, and your ministry will determine how high you go and how much weight of glory you carry. The choice is yours!

Increase and distinction comes through dedication.

What Is Dedication?

Dedication is defined as consecrated or set apart for service. For the anointing to increase in your life, your dedication to God, to your calling, and to your assignment are crucial. Your absolute and total dedication to God will determine your distinction in life.

Distinction is defined as excellence that sets someone or something apart from others. Or you can take hold of this definition: *"Distinction is that which causes you to stand out in honor."*

Your exploits in life and ministry are directly connected to your dedication to your call, church, ministry, or business. Your dedication is the price you will have to pay for greatness—your distinction. I know that's what you desire for your life and calling. Let's look at a very important event that took place when Solomon brought the ark of the covenant for the dedication of the temple of God. "And it came to pass, when the priests were come out of the holy place, that the cloud filled the house of the Lord" (1 Kings 8:10).

Your exploits in life and ministry are linked to your total dedication to God.

Notice the glory cloud filled the house. We know that the cloud was the glory. In Hebrews there are two main words for glory and they are:

❧ *Kabod,* which means heavily laden with good things, weighty, abundance, substance, splendor, riches, and esteemed position. Of course we all know the famous word *Ichabod,* meaning the glory has departed. Ichabod was the son of Phinehas. He was born on the day that the ark of God was taken into captivity by the Philistines. When his mother heard the shocking news that her husband and her father-in-law, Eli, had died and the ark of the covenant had been captured, she went into labor. Now pay close attention to the fact that the word *kabod* means weighty and heavy. This is very important.

❧ *Shekinah,* which means dwelling or settling. Although this word does not directly appear in the Scriptures, the concept clearly does and it is used to denote the dwelling or settling presence of God. It is derived from the Hebrew verb *shakan,* meaning to dwell. The Greek word *skene,* which also means dwelling, is thought to be derived from *shekinah* and *sakan.* The Jewish rabbis coined this extra biblical word to express the divine visitation of the presence or dwelling of God on a certain locality. For the Jews, it was the visible symbol of God's presence in the tabernacle, and later in Solomon's temple. The visible presence of God when He comes is the shekinah. 1 Kings 8:10-11 says:

It came to pass, when the priests were come out of the holy place, that the cloud filled the house of the Lord, so that the priests could not stand to minister because of the cloud: for the glory of the Lord had filled the house of the Lord.

I want you to note that when the temple was dedicated or yielded to God, the glory came and filled the house. The glory rested or weighted upon the house that was dedicated to God. Dedication releases glory!

Glory comes to the house
that is dedicated to God.

Life Application

~ The *temple* was a picture and a type of the believer, and it was also threefold. The three parts of the temple correspond to the triune state of man as stated by the apostle Paul in his first letter to the Thessalonians: "And the very God of peace sanctify you wholly; and I pray God your whole spirit and soul and body be preserved blameless unto the coming of our Lord Jesus Christ" (1 Thess. 5:23).

~ The *court*, which was outward and visible, represented the body.

~ The *holy place*, where everything appealed to the sacred emotions, represented the soul of man.

~ The *Holy of Holies*, the place of communion and presence of God represented the spirit of man.

~ The *ark of God* in the Holy of Holies was a type and shadow of God's presence and glory in our spirit and upon our lives.

Look at what the apostle Paul declares: "Know ye not that ye are the temple of God, and that the Spirit of God dwelleth in you?" (1 Cor. 3:16). Now we read, "What? Know ye not that your body is the temple of the Holy Ghost which is in you, which ye have of God, and ye are not your own? For ye are bought with a price: therefore glorify God in your body, and in your spirit, which are God's" (1 Cor. 6:19-20).

> You are anointed whether you feel like it or not simply because God said so in His Word.

Your body and spirit belong to God. Jesus' blood paid the price! Your body is the temple of God. In like manner, when you dedicate your body and life to God, His glory will fill your temple. After salvation comes dedication and consecration in order for us to see distinction. Salvation is your decision for initiation into the kingdom, but dedication takes a step toward distinction. In salvation Jesus becomes your Savior. In dedication Jesus truly becomes your Lord.

Your dedication to God will determine what you command. It will put you in a place of authority, power, and dominion. Moses' utmost dedication to God determined his command over Pharaoh, Jannes, and Jambres—the latter two, evil agents of witchcraft and the gods of Egypt. Daniel's dedication to God determined his command over the lions and warlocks of Persia. Paul's dedication to God determined his command over his enemies and life's circumstances. You must never forget this truth. Dedication will put you in a position of command and authority.

In Second Corinthians 4:17 we read, "For our light affliction, which is but for a moment, worketh for us a far more exceeding and eternal *weight of glory?"* Can you see that the word *weight* is associated with the word *glory.* Glory means that which is heavy therefore it has weight. It did not say the "height of glory," nor did it say "the distance of glory." It says the "weight of glory." In physics, weight is a measurement of the gravitational force acting on an object. The depth of your commitment to God will determine what *weight of glory* you will be able to carry.

Ask yourself these questions:

- How much anointing do you want to carry?
- How much glory do you want to carry?
- How much of God's presence do you want to carry?

All these and much more are determined by your dedication and commitment to God.

How Do I Dedicate Myself to God?

This is done by dedicating yourself to prayer, fasting, and study of the Word, yielding your body to God as an instrument of righteousness, and walking away from sin.

To What Do I Dedicate My Life?

You dedicate yourself to the call on your life and the ministry you have been given by God. Look at the words of the apostle Paul:

Rise, and stand upon thy feet: for I have appeared unto thee for this purpose, to make thee a minister and a witness both of these things which thou hast seen, and of those things in the which I will appear unto thee; delivering thee from the people, and from the Gentiles, unto whom now I send thee, to open their eyes, and to turn them from darkness to light, and from the power of Satan unto God, that they may receive forgiveness of sins, and inheritance among them which are sanctified by faith that is in Me. Whereupon, O king Agrippa, I was not disobedient unto the heavenly vision (Acts 26:16-19).

Stay dedicated to your field of ministry. Stop jumping around! One day you are a pastor, the next year you are an evangelist. Some people never bloom because they are never planted. Consider these scriptures:

- "Take heed to the ministry which thou hast received in the Lord, that thou fulfil it" (Col. 4:17).
- "Make full proof of thy ministry" (2 Tim. 4:5).
- "But contrariwise, when they saw that the gospel of the uncircumcision was committed unto me, as the gospel of the circumcision was unto Peter; (For He that wrought effectually in Peter to the apostleship of the circumcision, the same was mighty in me toward the Gentiles)" (Gal. 2:7-8).

Once you know what God has called you to do, dedicate your life to that service. Find out all the things that will make it work and that which will hinder it. If you keep doing what is right, it will grow. Dedicate your life to His service.

Chapter 13

BENEFITS OF
THE ANOINTING

As we discussed earlier in this book, the word *horn* refers to position and strength. In fact it refers to supernatural strength that elevates your position. God will exalt your position like the horn of a unicorn. Psalm 92:10-15 says:

> *My horn shalt Thou exalt like the horn of an unicorn: I shall be anointed with fresh oil. Mine eye also shall see my desire on mine enemies, and mine ears shall hear my desire of the wicked that rise up against me. The righteous shall flourish like the palm tree: he shall grow like a cedar in Lebanon. Those that be planted in the house of the Lord shall flourish in the courts of our God. They shall still bring forth fruit in old age; they shall be fat and flourishing; to shew that the Lord is upright: He is my rock, and there is no unrighteousness in Him.*

The literal translation says, "like the horn of a wild ox." Let us look at some of the benefits.

    ⚲ *Fortification—the anointing strengthens you.*

      "But my horn shalt Thou exalt like the horn of an unicorn: I shall be anointed with fresh oil" (Ps. 92:10).

"God brought them out of Egypt; he hath as it were *the strength of an unicorn [wild ox]*" (Num. 23:22).

❧ *Exaltation and Promotion.* The anointing will promote us, and God has no problem with that! The only thing God hates is when we try to exalt ourselves. But if we humble ourselves before Him, He will promote us. Consider these verses from the Psalms:

"But my horn shalt Thou exalt like the horn of an unicorn" (Ps. 92:10).

"You prepare a table before me in the presence of my enemies; You have anointed my head with oil; my cup overflows" (Ps. 23:5 NIV).

"You have loved righteousness and hated wickedness; therefore God, Your God, has anointed You with the oil of joy above Your fellows" (Ps. 45:7 NASB).

"And all the horns of the wicked He will cut off, but the horns of the righteous will be lifted up" (Ps. 75:10 NASB).

"For You are the glory of their strength, and by Your favor our horn is exalted" (Ps. 89:17 NASB).

"He has given freely to the poor, His righteousness endures forever; His horn will be exalted in honor" (Ps. 112:9 NASB).

❧ *Vision.* We are able to pick up the enemy's tracks and assignments. We will not be taken by surprise because we have insight into the plans of the wicked one.

"Mine eye also shall see my desire on mine enemies" (Ps. 92:11).

"I counsel thee to buy of me gold tried in the fire, that thou mayest be rich; and white raiment, that thou mayest be clothed, and that the shame of thy nakedness do not appear; and anoint thine eyes with eyesalve, that thou mayest see" (Rev. 3:18).

❧ *Perception/Instruction.* Our ears become sensitive to the voice of God. Just as the prophet Elisha knew every word that the king of Syria spoke in his bedroom and thwarted the plans of the enemies of Israel again and again, so God will open our ears to hear the plans of our enemies against us. As God opens our ears and gives us instructions, we will avoid the pitfalls, traps, and snares of satan. There will be no deception as we walk in the perception and instruction of God.

"And mine ears shall hear my desire of the wicked that rise up against me" (Ps. 92:11).

"For God speaketh once, yea twice, yet man perceiveth it not. In a dream, in a vision of the night, when deep sleep falleth upon men, in slumberings upon the bed; *then He openeth the ears of men, and sealeth their instruction,* that He may withdraw man from His purpose, and hide pride from man. He keepeth back his soul from the pit, and his life from perishing by the sword" (Job 33:14-18).

"And thine ears shall hear a word behind thee, saying, This is the way, walk ye in it, when ye turn to the right hand, and when ye turn to the left" (Isa. 30:21).

❧ *Station and multiplication.* With the anointing, our lives will flourish and multiply. In fact, there will be stability and multiplication in everything we do. Every work we set our hands to will prosper.

"The righteous shall flourish like the palm tree: he shall grow like a cedar in Lebanon. Those that be planted in the house of the Lord shall flourish in the courts of our God" (Ps. 92:12-13).

❧ *Production, generation, and rejuvenation.* Our best days are ahead of us. It doesn't matter how old we are, there will not be any barrenness in our lives. We will be fruitful, productive, and rejuvenated throughout all our days. The anointing will cause us to be fresh each day we spend upon the earth. We will still bring forth fruit.

"They shall still bring forth fruit in old age; they shall be fat and flourishing" (Ps. 92:14).

Declaration and confession. Anointed with fresh oil always gives us a fresh declaration. The devil will not be able to keep our mouths shut. We will be able to declare boldly of the goodness of God.

"To shew [declare] that the Lord is upright: He is my rock, and there is no unrighteousness in Him" (Ps. 92:15).

Chapter 14

GET READY
TO BE SALUTED

The encounter between Saul with Samuel the seer is fascinating. Samuel was anointing Saul as the first king of Israel. We read in 1 Samuel 10:1-6:

> *Samuel took a vial of oil, and poured it upon his head, and kissed him, and said, Is it not because the Lord hath anointed thee to be captain over His inheritance? When thou art departed from me to day, then thou shalt find two men by Rachel's sepulchre in the border of Benjamin at Zelzah; and they will say unto thee, The asses which thou wentest to seek are found: and, lo, thy father hath left the care of the asses, and sorroweth for you, saying, What shall I do for my son? Then shalt thou go on forward from thence, and thou shalt come to the plain of Tabor, and there shall meet thee three men going up to God to Bethel, one carrying three kids, and another carrying three loaves of bread, and another carrying a bottle of wine: And they will salute thee, and give thee two loaves of bread; which thou shalt receive of their hands. After that thou shalt come to the hill of God, where is the garrison of the Philistines: and it shall come to pass, when thou art come*

*thither to the city, that thou shalt meet a company of prophets
coming down from the high place with a psaltery, and a tabret,
and a pipe, and a harp, before them; and they shall prophesy:
And the Spirit of the Lord will come upon thee, and thou shalt
prophesy with them, and shalt be turned into another man.*

Saul's Experience Can Be Your Prophecy

Before his encounter with Samuel, the Bible says Saul was looking
for the lost donkeys of his father. Look at First Samuel 9:3-4 NIV:

*Now the donkeys belonging to Saul's father Kish were lost,
and Kish said to his son Saul, "Take one of the servants with
you and go and look for the donkeys." So he passed through
the hill country of Ephraim and through the area around
Shalisha, but they did not find them. They went on into the
district of Shaalim, but the donkeys were not there. Then he
passed through the territory of Benjamin, but they did not
find them.*

Saul and one of his servants had been searching for the lost donkeys for three days and still could not find them. They had walked all
over the place to no avail. Now, in our Western mind-set, we don't attach much value to donkeys, but in those days, donkeys were a sign of
wealth and finances. Consequently, lost donkeys would mean lost
wealth. Saul must have been sweating as he and his father's servant
checked every nook and cranny for those wayward beasts.

It may be that you find yourself in the same predicament Saul was
in. You are searching for your Father's inheritance. It may be that
your wealth has been taken away from you and no matter how hard
you try you cannot get your breakthrough. You may have been pacing
up and down like Saul, searching everywhere and finding nothing.

Saul's story changed when he had an appointment with the
anointing. Your story is about to change as you have an encounter
with the anointing of God. You are about to rewrite your history. This
is God's prophecy to you.

168

Be the Captain

"Then Samuel took a vial of oil, and poured it upon his head, and kissed him, and said, Is it not because the Lord hath *anointed thee to be captain* over His inheritance?" (1 Sam. 10:1).

You have been anointed to become the captain and leader in whatever field you are in. Do you realize that Saul came from the smallest tribe and the family of least status? Your background has no bearing on your future. From today, understand the anointing is resident in you to make you the president.

℗ *Through the anointing,* God is taking you out of the land of obscurity into the land of visibility.

℗ *Through the anointing,* God is taking you out of insignificance and into prominence.

℗ *Through the anointing,* God is taking you from being overlooked to being an overcomer.

℗ *Through the anointing,* God is taking you out of darkness and into the light.

You may have started out as nothing, but God has anointed you to be someone special, a person of significance.

Your Inheritance Restored

"When thou art departed from me to day, then thou shalt find two men by Rachel's sepulchre in the border of Benjamin at Zelzah; and they will say unto thee, *the asses which thou wentest to seek are found*" (1 Sam. 10:2).

Saul's days of pacing up and down to no avail came to an abrupt end. From after today, your days of pacing up and down with no breakthroughs will be over as well. That which you could not find in your natural strength will be restored to you through the anointing of God.

Some of you have given up on inheritance that your parents left you. Let me prophesy in your life, "There will be a recovery of all in your life." Whatever you sought without the anointing and could not appropriate will come to your life and hands. Whatever eluded you in years gone by will come in to your hands this year. Believe it and take it.

Progress from this Day Forward

"Then shalt thou go on forward from thence" (1 Sam. 10:3). From this day forward, there will be major advancement in your life. You will no longer be in reverse gear. You are now in "forward" gear and hell cannot stop you. Satan cannot stop you, and your enemies cannot stop you. You are marching forward. Make these confessions:

- *From today,* your life is going forward and not backward.
- *From today,* your ministry is progressing and not regressing.
- *From today,* your finances are going up and not down.

Prosperity and Covenant Joy

"Thou shalt come to the plain of Tabor, and there shall meet thee three men going up to God to Bethel, one carrying three kids, and another carrying three loaves of bread, and another carrying a bottle of wine" (1 Sam. 10:3).

Since you are anointed, people will no longer overlook you and bless others in your stead. People will come from all over the city and nations of the world to pour into your life. Everything that hid your face from people to bless you is now removed and financial seeds are coming to your life. People are hunting you down just to bless you.

Get Ready to Be Saluted!

"*They will salute thee,* and give thee two loaves of bread; which thou shalt receive of their hands" (1 Sam. 10:4).

The day before, Saul had been an unknown, but after his encounter with Samuel and his anointing, he gained notoriety. One day he was a nobody from the smallest tribe and the least family, and then the next he was God's anointed king. The day before, no one thought to salute Saul, but after his anointing, all the people saluted him. Those who resented him and those who had spoken badly of him all had to stand and salute.

This will happen in your life as well. Those who have mocked you will be made to stand and salute you, regardless of how they feel about you. They will be required to respect the position where God has placed you. Notice that the passage says, "*...and you shall receive of their hands.*" Whatever hands were closed to you before will now be open to you.

Be the Different Man

After that thou shalt come to the hill of God, where is the garrison of the Philistines: and it shall come to pass, when thou art come thither to the city, that thou shalt meet a company of prophets coming down from the high place with a psaltery, and a tabret, and a pipe, and a harp, before them; and they shall prophesy: And the Spirit of the Lord will come upon thee, and thou shalt prophesy with them, and shalt be turned into another man (1 Samuel 10:5-6).

The Spirit of God is upon you and you, are no longer what you used to be. You are a different man, a different woman. The anointing has made the difference!

CONTACT THE AUTHOR

Glenn Arekion Ministries

PO Box 72672
Louisville, KY 40272
USA

mail@glennarekion.org
www.glennarekion.org